WORKING WITH SENSITIZING CONCEPTS: ANALYTICAL FIELD RESEARCH

p.5 symbolic interactionism
p.30 sensitizing concept & ccm

WILL C. van den HOONAARD
University of New Brunswick

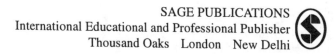

Qualitative Research Methods
Volume 41

D1248616

SAGE PUBLICATIONS
International Educational and Professional Publisher
Thousand Oaks   London   New Delhi

For information address:

 SAGE Publications, Inc.
2455 Teller Road
Thousand Oaks, California 91320
Phone: 805-499-0721
E-mail: order@sagepub.com

SAGE Publications Ltd.
6 Bonhill Street
London EC2A 4PU
United Kingdom

SAGE Publications India Pvt. Ltd.
M-32 Market
Greater Kailash I
New Delhi 110 048 India

Printed in the United States of America

Library of Congress Cataloging-in-Publication Data

Hoonaard, Will C. van den, 1942-
    Working with sensitizing concepts: Analytical field research /
author, Will C. van den Hoonaard.
        p.   cm.—(Qualitative research methods; v. 41)
    Includes bibliographical references.
    ISBN 0-7619-0206-6 (cloth: acid-free paper).—ISBN
0-7619-0207-4 (pbk.: acid-free paper)
        1. Social sciences—Research—Methodology. 2. Social sciences—
Fieldwork. I. Title. II. Series.
    H62.H598   1996
    300′.72—dc20   96-25242

This book is printed on acid-free paper.

97   98   99   00   01   02   10   9   8   7   6   5   4   3   2   1

Acquiring Editor: Peter Labella
Editorial Assistant: Frances Borghi
Production Editor: Michèle Lingre
Production Assistant: Sherrise Purdum
Typesetter/Designer: Andrea D. Swanson/Dick Palmer

CONTENTS

Dedicated to
Deborah Kestin van den Hoonaard

SERIES EDITORS' INTRODUCTION

The sensitizing concept is a solution to the vexing problem of making sense of fieldnotes and observations once in the analysis stage. The utility of a sensitizing concept, as conceived by Herbert Blumer, was to make possible the transition from actors' understandings and meanings to analytic, generalizing concepts. Blumer thus introduced a concept and an explicit approach to data analysis: remain true to the empirical world of the actors. Qualitative work, as van den Hoonaard shows, requires working through real concrete data to sensitizing concepts to generalizations. This goes to the heart of qualitative data analysis: making sense of the social space where data and concepts collide.

This contribution to the **Sage Qualitative Research Methods Series** (41st volume) outlines Blumer's ideas; the range of sensitizing concepts; illustrates their many uses in his own fieldwork, and connects the idea to social science theory in a final chapter.

Because it moves skillfully from concept to theory and data and back, it shares territory with other volumes in the Series, such as Feldman's work on strategies for interpreting qualitative data, Altheide's on qualitative media analysis, and Wolcott's on writing up field data. It continues the focus of the Series on explicating qualitative analysis.

—Peter K. Manning
John Van Maanen
Marc L. Miller

PREFACE

I suspect that readers who are new to the world of qualitative research have picked up this book because they are attracted to the term "sensitizing," rather than to "concepts," in the book's title. If my suspicions are true, it is because there is a desire among these readers to *understand* the "native perspective," and what better avenue than *sensitizing* oneself to that perspective? This is what long-haul practitioners have seen when using sensitizing concepts. With even modest training in the use of sensitizing concepts, I believe that graduate students can gain sociological insights that previously seemed to be blocked by more elegant theories and approaches. This book is about making both the world of the native perspective and the world of theory less intimidating.

I owe my interest in ethnographic work to my teacher Nels Anderson, who guided me with his exhortation, "You can't be a sociologist if you look *down* at the sidewalk! Look around, take note, and take notes." Along the way, ethnographic research has shifted from being a descriptive science to one more theoretical in focus. It is to this shift—the rebirth of qualitative research, with a special interest in theoretical analysis—that I owe the present volume.

It was, however, a fieldnotes presentation by Dr. Uldis Kundrats of Nipissing University, on learning to play the blues, at the 1994 Qualitative Analysis Meetings at the University of Waterloo, Ontario, that explicitly laid the foundation of this particular volume. I felt impelled to keep fieldnotes during my sessions with a speech therapist, Ms. Cynthia Howroth of the Speech Institute in Fredericton, New Brunswick, Canada. In the course of my taking fieldnotes, a sensitizing concept, *detective work*, emerged from the debris of data. When I realized that there exists no publication that specifically deals with sensitizing concepts, I approached Dr. John Van Maanen, the chief Series Editor of the Qualitative Research Methods Series, and asked whether it would be of any use for me to write a monograph on the subject. The current monograph represents the culmination of the enthusiastic reception by Dr. John Van Maanen and the active support given by Mr. Peter Labella, the Sage Editor.

I owe a particularly large debt to Dr. Noel Iverson of the University of New Brunswick's Department of Sociology for his guidance and assistance in examining the underpinnings of this volume. Several ideas in this monograph were cultivated at the University of New Brunswick in a graduate seminar on research design during the fall of 1994. The students provided a healthy dose of critique and encouragement. Particular mention, however, should be made of Ms. Linda Turner and Ms. Karen Hutton, who, in their attempts to develop several sensitizing concepts for their doctoral research, have generously offered their insights and approaches. Dr. Peter K. Manning provided the necessary reader's review to bring the manuscript closer to publication. Ms. Sherry L. Dupuis, a doctoral candidate at the University of Guelph, shared with me her critique of a very early draft of the manuscript. Dr. Paul McDonnell of the Psychology Department at the University of New Brunswick also offered valuable assistance. I have found a rich source of provocative material on the subject of sensitizing concepts. John and Lyn Lofland's *Analyzing Social Settings* (1995) was particularly useful in that respect. Ms. Carla Balcom, an undergraduate in our department, provided her meticulous research skills when I asked for her assistance in this project. I am grateful for her help.

I am deeply indebted to Dr. Deborah Kestin van den Hoonaard, whose expertise and insights on qualitative research methods, resulting from her own extensive research on Florida retirement communities and widows, I value very highly. Both generous with her ideas and insightful in her sociology, she has brought me closer to qualitative research than any other person. I have looked forward to dedicating this monograph to her. It should be borne in mind, however, that the dedication of a book stands far removed from any of the imperfections that may characterize the manuscript.

A Note About Gender, Language, and Research "Subjects"

Many readers will, I hope, agree that the current debates and struggles about gender and language have convinced researchers and others to incorporate both women and men in language, description, and analysis. The reader is, no doubt, aware that in citing older works, we come across masculine forms of language that were intended to address either men, or men and women. I am not inclined to pepper these older quotations with parenthetical "and/or her" notations and the like. For one thing, this approach, when practiced indiscriminately, makes it harder to read these older works. The reader should be aware that, unless I have indicated otherwise, I have meant these cited works to signify also women, *mutandis mutandi*. I have also adopted the practice of alternating chapters in referring to women or men in an effort to make the text less cumbersome. I warmly endorse Margit Eichler's work (1988) for those who want to explore further the issues of gender and research.

Something should be said about the term "research subjects." I have always found the terms "subjects" and "respondents" awkward and un-yielding. The term "participants" strikes me as insincere in some, but not all, research work. Particularly in sociological work in the 1960s and 1970s, one comes across "actor," which, I take it, is used in a narrow technical sense to refer to someone who undertakes any activity, whether mental or physical. I make use of all these terms, depending on the points being discussed.

WORKING WITH SENSITIZING CONCEPTS: Analytical Field Research

WILL C. van den HOONAARD
University of New Brunswick

1. BACKGROUND AND HISTORY

Anyone stepping into the world of doing qualitative research sooner or later realizes that qualitative work encompasses an extensive range of approaches, from content analysis to life-history narratives. What is common to the whole range is the following well-known premise, which Herbert Blumer so clearly articulates:

> The first premise is that human beings act toward things on the basis of the meanings that the things have for them. Such things include everything that the human being may note in the world. . . . The second premise is that the meaning of such things is derived from, or arises out of, the social interaction that one has with one's fellows [*sic*]. The third premise is that these meanings are handled in, and modified through, an interpretive process used by the person in dealing with the things he encounters. (Blumer, 1969, p. 2)

The sensitizing concept is a construct that is derived from the research participants' perspective, uses their language or expression, and sensitizes the researcher to possible lines of inquiry. Some concepts are provisional, whereas others have a longer staying power. The sensitizing concept seems a logical, and even necessary, methodological consequence of Blumer's fundamental premise; the sensitizing concept is a meaning that naturally arises among the people we study (cf. Berg, 1995, p. 24). The sensitizing concept allows us to see those meanings that people attach to the world around them. A sensitizing concept "gives the user a general sense of reference and guidance in approaching empirical instances . . . [and] merely suggest[s] directions along which to look" (Blumer, 1954, p. 7). What better way of capturing such meanings than by using the sensitizing concept, which, if properly constructed, contains the words and thoughts that research subjects attach to their world?

What led me to write this monograph on sensitizing concepts was their efficacy in helping me sort through my fieldnotes and interview transcriptions during a life of research that started with an Icelandic participant observational study in 1970. Moreover, both graduate and undergraduate students have, over the years, responded with enthusiasm and new insights about their own research after having learned more about sensitizing concepts. I believe that we can acquire a fuller appreciation of these types of concepts only when we consider their historical underpinnings and current trends among social scientists.

Early in 1954, Herbert Blumer lifted a hand against the prevailing modes of social theory, namely functionalism and psychologism. He identified their "grave shortcomings" in their "glaring" separation from the empirical world (Blumer, 1954, p. 3). His 4,300-word classic essay, titled "What Is Wrong With Social Theory?" decries the aridity of theories removed many times from the empirical world. For Herbert Blumer, as Leon and Diana Warshay (1986, p. 181) remind us, the "macro formulations in terms of social systems, cultural demands, and institutional stresses omitted people as actors by treating them as 'carriers' who are irrelevant."[1] No longer satisfied with the then-current "conspicuously defective" theory, Herbert Blumer etched a simple methodological approach that would prove remarkably effective in both capturing empirical data and generating theory.[2]

Blumer's own answer to what he perceived to be the failings of the social theory of the time was the *sensitizing concept*. A sensitizing concept is a

starting point in thinking about a class of data of which the social researcher has no definite idea and provides an initial guide to her research. Such concepts usually are provisional and may be dropped as more viable and definite concepts emerge in the course of her research.

Such a concept allows the researcher to sensitize herself conveniently to a particular category of data about which she initially knows little. The intent is to highlight the unique properties of those data. Sensitizing concepts are useful when we do not know enough about a social setting or group of people to "identify relevant problems and hypotheses" (Becker, 1958, p. 653). For example, Deborah van den Hoonaard uses the concept of *identity foreclosure* to refer to a situation in which new widows find themselves. This concept permits us to take into account social data that seem to point to the foreclosure of one's identity:

> Identity foreclosure refers to the fact that, although [widows] try to hang onto their identities as wives, they no longer have the social resources to do so. They find themselves symbolically stranded on the sidewalk with their belongings (i.e. the elements of their identity) strewn about them. This results in a loss of self. (van den Hoonaard, 1995b, p. 1)

The sensitizing concept can be used as a "general sense of reference and guidance" in approaching empirical data, uniting the empirical and social worlds:

> If our empirical world presents itself in the form of distinctive and unique happenings or situations and if we seek through the direct study of this world to establish classes of objects, we are, I think, forced to work with sensitizing concepts. (Blumer, 1954, p. 8)[3]

In short, the sensitizing concept gives us a general sense of reference and guides us in approaching empirical instances. Moreover, it suggests "directions along which to look" (Blumer, 1954, p. 7). The sensitizing concept also is a "second-order" concept that is one more step removed from the data, but using, as much as warranted, the perspective of the research participants. Sociologists use the sensitizing concept as a "construct of constructs," as a deliberate ploy to generate theory. The sensitizing supra-concept, such as *community,* speaks to a larger body of data but is similarly used to generate theory.

Blumer did not intend these concepts to be definitive in the manner of offering a clear-cut identification of a particular class of data. For him, there is a beneficial advantage of using *sensitizing* concepts rather than *definitive* ones. Because sensitizing concepts do not create closure during one's research, he thought they would be most useful in studying empirical instances. The term "assimilation," for example, encompasses a variety of empirical events that are given shape by circumstances peculiar to the situation. Such an inductive approach to the study of micro phenomena allows one to derive generic statements "from the ongoing symbolic processes of individuals in concrete interaction situations" (Turner, 1978, p. 401). Elaborating on what C. Wright Mills characterizes as Concepts with a capital "C," sensitizing concepts are written with a lowercase *c*. Concepts involve the "arid game," declares Mills (1959, p. 34), of unimaginative Grand Theory, whereas concepts indicate the fluid character of social investigation and the researcher's listening to the explanations that respondents make about their own social world.

Rather than having an abstract framework embrace the empirical instance, it is the "concrete distinctiveness" of empirical events that gives shape to the sensitizing concept (Blumer, 1954, p. 8). Blumer summons for us the image of an unknown social terrain that, like a landscape, must be traversed. Our trained eyes allow us to see the basic cartographic features on a map: the contours of mountains and rivers that allow us to speculate about possible passes or trails. As these cartographic features get us closer to the actual empirical instance, we discern further peculiarities of the terrain. Our tentative notions of the landscape alert us to the possibilities of traveling through the terrain. The particular, concrete expression of the landscape molds our concept of it and, through the concept, allows us to find instances of it in other types of landscapes.

Blumer's 1954 call for the use of the sensitizing concept resolved his 23-year concern about concepts of science and of common sense (Baugh, 1990, pp. 10-11).[4] Concepts that mimicked the natural sciences, he believed, were too removed from the world of experience and were manufactured "recklessly," without regard to their need. He believed that such concepts, moreover, tended to terminate inquiry, because to "label something with a concept is to explain it" (Baugh, 1990, p. 11). "Abstracted empiricism" is how one other thinker of the 1950s, C. Wright Mills, described the manipulation of data to conform to measurement (Mills, 1959, pp. 50-51).

Finally, one tends to loosely understand concepts in social science, rather than to have a clear meaning of them. Blumer's 1940 article, "The Problem of the Concept in Social Psychology," already claimed that the gap between theory and observation constitutes a major dilemma in social psychological research (Baugh, 1990, pp. 20-21). According to Blumer, social psychologists not only constructed an atheoretical empiricism but also invented concepts that are hard to validate empirically.[5]

We should make an explicit connection between Blumer's general approach to the study of human interaction and his specific use of the sensitizing concept to George H. Mead and symbolic interactionism. One can extract the nub, or the germ, of what makes the use of the sensitizing concept such a natural ally in symbolic interactionist work from what Blumer has said about Mead's approach to the social world:

[T]he human being [has ceased to be regarded as] a responding organism whose behavior is a product of what plays upon him from the outside, the inside, or both. Instead, he acts toward his world, interpreting what confronts him and organizing his action on the basis of the interpretation. . . . [This] process puts the human being over against his world instead of merely in it, [and] requires him to meet and handle his world through a defining process instead of merely responding to it. (Blumer, 1966, p. 536)

What we thus require is a methodology that takes into account this "defining process." What better technique than the use of the sensitizing concept?

The concerns sketched in the previous paragraph have occupied the minds of other scholars. Alfred Schutz (1970, p. 11), for example, stressed the danger of concepts being "remote from the obvious and familiar traits found in any society" and commended an approach that "agree[s] with the commonsense experience of the social world," because it stands to reason that social reality "has a specific meaning and relevance structure for the human beings living, acting and thinking within it."

The *sensitizing concept* articulates Blumer's particular approach and, despite the criticism (and Blumer's own "controversial advocacy") of such concepts (Shibutani, 1988, p. 29), sociologists have given virtually silent support for the use of sensitizing concepts, both directly and indirectly. Symbolic interactionists and like-minded researchers are now rediscovering the richness of Blumer's works (Fine, 1990, p. 147). A special issue on Herbert Blumer's legacy of *Symbolic Interaction* (Spring, 1988) speaks eloquently to Blumer's widespread contribution to the study of human interaction. Following are five illustrations of the ways that the sensitizing concept has seeped into sociological practice.

First, despite their invisibility, we find sensitizing concepts used in several areas of current sociological research, sometimes without their being named as such. For example, the defining characteristic of Barney Glaser and Anselm Strauss's "grounded theory" (1967, p. 1), directed toward the "discovery of theory from data," is a direct descendant of Blumer's sensitizing concept. John Lofland (1970, p. 38) regards their *The Discovery of Grounded Theory* as a "plea for the development of mini-concepts" by setting out the procedures to invent such concepts. Glaser and Strauss use the term "category" to refer to the sensitizing concept (e.g., 1967, p. 25), preferring to reserve the notion of *concept* for a higher level of abstraction. Much like Blumer in the 1950s, who reacted against functionalism and psychologism, Glaser and Strauss railed against Merton's "middle-range," a priori, theories and argued that the groups, settings, and methods cannot be specified at the start of one's research (Hammersley, 1989, p. 173). In such an approach, theoretical ideas emerge as the research moves forward. Like the spirit that animates the use of the sensitizing concept, Glaser and Strauss caution us not to lose our "potential theoretical sensitivity," lest we become insensitive and defensive toward new insights derived from data (1967, p. 46). In *Patterns of Discovery in the Social Sciences*, Paul Diesing sees sensitizing concepts as the "basic component of holistic theories" (1971, p. 209). In psychology, it might be noted that the concept of the *resilient child* acts as a sensitizing concept (Zimmerman & Arunkumar, 1994).

Second, although he never labeled himself an interactionist, we must include Erving Goffman as a key developer of sensitizing concepts on account of his strengths in microsociology (Collins, 1994, p. 277). If we exclude him, Gary Fine claims, we "exclude our soul" (1990, p. 121).[6] Others would describe Goffman as the "champion inventor of the mini-concept," responding to the "barrenness of the conceptual landscape" (Lofland, 1970, p. 38). It was Goffman's obsession with sensitizing concepts that led one scholar to exclaim that Goffman "has more concepts than there are referents" (Lofland, 1970, p. 38). Glaser and Strauss report that he was "among the most prolific inventors of concepts in sociology" (Glaser & Strauss, 1967, p. 136).

Goffman seems to have gone through two phases in his scholarship. The first phase is a descendant of Durkheimian theory of rituals, and the second is a counterpoint to Garfinkel's ethnomethodology (Collins, 1994, p. 277). It was during the first phase that Goffman delivered some of the more memorable and lively depictions of interaction rituals that can be seen as echoes of the sensitizing concept.[7] His study of interactional behavior has claimed the interest of many students and sociologists, and even the wider public.

Third, the development of the focus group as a sociological tool has roots in Blumer's advocacy of "discussion or resource groups" as a path in developing sensitizing concepts (Blumer, 1969, p. 41). He believed that such groups'

> discussing collectively their sphere of life and probing into it as they meet one another's disagreements [would] do more to lift the veils covering the sphere of life than any other device that I know of. (Blumer, 1969, p. 41)

Focus groups consist of a small number of people, let us say 10, who are brought together by the investigator for one or more of these reasons: drawing out information about selected topics of interest to the researcher, replacing a series of interviews that for lack of time cannot be undertaken, and coming up with ideas and solutions (Berg, 1995, pp. 68-69). As David Morgan reminds us, focus groups had their origins in sociology, with the work of Robert K. Merton and Patricia L. Kendall in 1946, although market research has found them particularly useful (Morgan, 1988, pp. 10, 11). Although Blumer was not the first to use the term "focus group," his deep and urgent interest in using focus groups to stimulate the development of sensitizing concepts brought the term to a broader sociological audience.

Fourth, the discipline has witnessed in recent years a flood of works that fosters both conventional and newer qualitative scholarship. The production of an abundance of qualitative methods texts and the so-called "new" ethnographies reflect this development. These "new" ethnographies highlight, among other things, a greater relevance of theory (Fine, 1990, p. 131).[8] There is now an urgency to provide a more lively theory that can shed light on ethnographic data and transform the data into viable concepts. As a whole, the new ethnographies, with their heavier emphasis on theory, seem to reflect John Lofland's assessment that until 1970 (when he published "Interactionist Imagery and Analytic Interruptus"), the work of symbolic interactionists had veered away from considering theory as a component of research (Lofland, 1970, p. 37). In any event, the reemergence in past years of qualitative research perspectives and controversies (Falk & Anderson, 1983, p. 23) has led to the need both to train a new generation of researchers and to help them reassess the classical approaches to doing qualitative research, in addition to the more deliberate theoretical infusion of such research. The current volume is an outgrowth of such reassessments. As Van Maanen (1988, p. xi) avers, we "seem to be in a period of considerable uncertainty and change. . . . New voices are audible, new styles are visible, and new puzzles are being put forth." Norman K. Denzin's (1992) efforts in "cultural studies" bring to mind one of symbolic interactionists' most vigorous efforts to merge symbolic interactionism with the insights of contemporary cultural studies and feminism.

Fifth, the use of the sensitizing concept is so widespread and commonplace that many social scientists today no longer feel the need to articulate their indebtedness to Blumer. Virtually no introductory textbooks in sociology, and not even methodological textbooks, make explicit reference to the sensitizing concept. *The Encyclopedia of Sociology* (1981) carries no reference to sensitizing concepts. Some textbooks that explicitly adopt the qualitative research approach ignore sensitizing concepts. In other words, the success of sensitizing concepts is so widespread that it has, ironically, become invisible. More specifically, we might mention the appearance of

Doing Everyday Life (Dietz, Prus, & Shaffir, 1994), *Qualitative Research Methods for the Social Sciences* (Berg, 1995), and a second edition of *Qualitative Data Analysis* (Miles & Huberman, 1994), which omit references to sensitizing concepts. There are others (e.g., Agar, 1980; Kirby & McKenna, 1989; Lofland & Lofland, 1995; Shaffir, Stebbins, & Turowetz, 1980), but a happy and cogent exception is *Constructing Social Research*, in which Charles Ragin (1994, pp. 87-88) developed two succinct but well-defined explanations of sensitizing concepts.

Contemporary bureaucratic settings, ironically, offer the best evidence for the hidden success of sensitizing concepts. Here, concepts are deliberately used to shift attention away from the problematic nature of social problems. A *surgical airstrike*, for example, is deliberated constructed to convey both a "clean" and necessary bomb drop. The concepts of *friendly fire* and *collateral damage*, indicating artillery fire from one's own troops and the taking of human life by air-raid bombs, respectively, offer the most extreme use of sensitizing concepts. In these instances, the concepts force us to desensitize ourselves to social reality.

As modern society is increasingly governed by "explicit processes of interpretation rather than by traditional norms" (Hammersley, 1989, p. 116), it stands to reason that the study of the use of sensitizing concepts should become increasingly relevant. Blumer, along with a few others in the 1950s, anticipated a world contrived by bureaucrats as a "world of facts to be treated in accordance with firm rules" (Mills, 1959, p. 117). Manipulation and ideological justification characterize such worlds; our use of sensitizing concepts, I believe, is a humble effort to recognize the world experienced by people as real, enduring, ever changing, and fraught with meaning. The larger purpose that sustains the use of sensitizing concepts is the desire to see human beings as "sentient, experiencing, passionate creatures" (Reinharz, 1993, p. 36), eschewing methodological rigidity but welcoming people back into sociology. I have written this monograph with the aim of offsetting what Nielsen terms the "enlightened ruthlessness that comes from the actual practice of empirical research" (1984, p. 1241). In our eagerness to do research, to find theoretical frameworks, we can overlook the people whose lives we are researching and replace our eagerness with "enlightened ruthlessness."

This monograph will explore the sensitizing concept from a variety of angles, some of them overlapping. A reawakening of sensitizing concepts as tools for transforming data into theory indicates a need to examine the criticisms of using sensitizing concepts (Chapter 2). An appreciation of those criticisms allows us to appreciate the strengths, weaknesses, and usefulness of these concepts. Chapter 3 places the sensitizing concept in the debate about the implications of using concepts as a means of maintaining distance from the data and considers the characteristics of colloquial expressions and sensitizing concepts. This chapter offers a useful heuristic figure that locates sensitizing concepts in the context of other, roughly similar, concepts. Chapter 4 is a "how to" approach in constructing the sensitizing concept. Chapter 5 offers a practical demonstration of how sensitizing concepts are constructed, drawing on the author's fieldwork experience in Iceland. Chapter 6 considers some of the theoretical and analytical contributions of the sensitizing concept, both as a qualitative research tool and as a link to wider theories.

NOTES

1. Some, like Morrione (1988, p. 7) take issue with the Warshays' other claims that Blumer was a "subjectivist." I am inclined to agree with Morrione when he says that, for Blumer, analysis connoted a joint action (of the subject and observer). Maines (1988, p. 45) joins Morrione in his critique of the Warshays' argument.

2. Chapter 5 in Hammersley (1989), "Against the Trend: Blumer's Critique of Quantitative Method," provides a more detailed analysis of Blumer's position.

3. Hammersley (1989, pp. 123-125) gives a concise overview of Blumer's ideas of definitive and sensitizing concepts.

4. *Symbolic Interactionism: Perspective and Method* (Blumer, 1969) contains Blumer's important articles dealing with sensitizing concepts (but also with his approach and methodology involving symbolic interactionism). A number of the articles do not contain information about their original publication.

5. Since the time that Blumer made these comments, there have been a number of major theoretical advances in psychology through the use of concepts in learning theory, cognitive dissonance, and social comparison theory.

6. There are others, however, who are firm in their assessment that Goffman is no symbolic interactionist (Bolton, 1981, p. 697). Collins goes as far as saying that Goffman never regarded the symbolic interactionists as "intellectually very serious" (Collins, 1994, p. 277). This debate, no doubt, will be the source of many theses.

7. Goffman's *Asylums* (1961a) uses at least 81 concepts (or one for every 4.8 pages), whereas *Interaction Ritual* (1967), which includes his classic essay, "Where the Action Is," contains 77 concepts, or one for every 3.5 pages. *Encounters* (1961b) includes the seminal chapter on *role distance* and provides some 48 examples of such concepts, or one concept per 3.2 pages. In *Presentation of Self in Everyday Life* (1959), Goffman uses 103 sensitizing concepts, or one for every 2.5 pages.

8. The recent formalization of "social constructionism" in sociology is but one facet of these developments.

2. THE CRITICS

Perhaps not unlike the reader who is currently learning more about what it means to be a social scientist and a scholar, I have gravitated toward learning more about the objections that others have toward a particular field or approach in which I have an interest. Critics can thus be a helpful part of the learning process.

Before I turn to discussing the merits and possibilities of using the sensitizing concept, we need to have a clear understanding of the force of criticisms leveled against its use in research. This is precisely what I have in mind in this chapter. Understanding the criticisms allows us to appreciate, or even improve, the good use of the sensitizing concept.

The reception of Blumer's proposal was, given the context of the times, cool, to say the least. Some, like Howard S. Becker (1988, p. 15), aver that his ideas "provoked violent, angry responses" from those whose framework he challenged. We hear of Stouffer denouncing him as "the gravedigger of American sociology" (Becker, 1988, p. 15). But who is better remembered: Samuel Stouffer or Herbert Blumer? Even today, there are those who have difficulty in accepting his ideas. Kenneth Baugh, Jr., in *The Methodology of Herbert Blumer: Critical Interpretation and Repair* (1990, pp. 26-32), devotes a special section to the "rise and *fall* of the 'sensitizing concept' " (italics added). Some claim that Blumer himself apparently had abandoned its use after 1956 (Baugh, 1990, p. 32). Other critics have made erroneous assumptions about his distinctive emphasis on emergent social action.[1] For his part, Blumer has reciprocated by characterizing the views of his opponents as "absurd" (Blumer, 1973, p. 798). Whatever the criticisms of Blumer's methodology, they were framed as a function of the political factions within sociology at the time, namely the "Chicago school of sociology" versus the "East Coast sociology," spearheaded by Robert K. Merton, Talcott Parsons, and others, which decried "subjective" sociology in favor of macrostructural, scientistic, and "objective" approaches.

A central weakness of the criticism directed against Blumer and his notion of the sensitizing concept is the profound lack of recognition of Blumer's fundamental point that (social) reality exists in relation to other things, that the meaning of that reality is given in terms of these relations, and that the relatedness of things is constantly moving and dynamic (Morrione, 1988, p. 6). We can organize the claims of such critics as Kenneth Baugh, Jr., and others into six areas, namely that sensitizing concepts:

1. diverge from Blumer's social science procedure,
2. do not consider social structural features,
3. are vague,
4. are nominal definitions,
5. restrict the breadth of data that can be collected, and
6. can go stale.

This chapter will consider each of these criticisms. It will be important to remember, as will be evident from the following sections, that some of the criticisms have not been motivated by a desire to improve the use of sensitizing concepts and that some of the critics are staunch positivists. This list of criticisms stems from my reading of the literature that proffered a critical stance toward the use of sensitizing concepts. Six themes emerged from this literature, which ranges from constructive to hostile.

Sensitizing Concepts as Anomalies in Blumer's Social Scientific Procedure

In the light of criticisms directed at Blumer's notion of the sensitizing concept, it is important for us to decide whether such criticisms are with, or without, foundation. If these criticisms can be substantiated, we are forced to rely on a smaller body of Blumer's *oeuvre* to understand the nature, purpose, and use of the sensitizing concept than is the case otherwise.

If we were to rely on commentators, it would be hard to gauge whether Blumer's key 1931 article, "Science Without Concepts," either laid the methodological foundation of his future work or is a contrast to it. This article advocates the use of scientific concepts that, at once, abstract from experience and make it possible to anticipate new, theoretical, insights about empirical data. The Chicago school of sociology—with which Blumer stands identified—provided, even in the early 1930s, very little information about how social research was to be carried out (Hammersley, 1989, pp. 84-85).[2] Specifically, to what extent does Blumer's later formulation of sensitizing concepts affirm or deny the ideas in the 1931 article?

Some, like Baugh (1990, p. 31), see sensitizing concepts as departing in important ways from both Blumer's earlier and later methodological approaches.[3] According to Baugh, Blumer advocated in 1955 that concepts must point to the individual instances of the class of empirical objects to which they refer, although in 1931 Blumer had favored, following Baugh, a more loose, commonsense approach, sensing one's way to the study of social relations.

Charles Tucker clarified in his essay "Herbert Blumer: A Pilgrimage With Pragmatism" (1988, p. 112) that Blumer underwent a slight shift in his methodological position, from emphasizing pragmatism to highlighting the "empiric." All the same, Tucker confirms that it was Blumer's 1931 article that laid the foundation for his later social scientific work and that his earlier work "show[s] a dominant interest in applying and perpetuating pragmatism" (Tucker, 1988, pp. 106-107).[4] Moreover, in Tucker's view, Blumer "refused" to accept the judgment of many social scientists, including those who were sympathetic to him, that he had moved away from pragmatism and the scientific framework. In any event, Tucker avers that, despite Blumer's attempts to allay the misgivings of his opponents, he resorted to polemics (and some would use the pejorative term "scholasticism") and that, in the end, he was not able to answer his critics (Tucker, 1988, p. 118).

Joan Huber, a fervent positivist who seems to neither understand nor appreciate Blumer's approach, directs her criticism at the fact that sensitizing concepts lack "specific objective benchmarks." For her, there is little, if any, "specification of the rules of logic or procedure to be used" (Huber, 1973, p. 280). Moreover, as Blumer urges the use of well-informed observers in pointing out the empirical referents for this or that sensitizing concept, Huber raises the specter of observers' failing to agree on the view taken by the researcher and of having no assurance that the researcher is either objective or reliable. It troubles Huber that the social scientist's use of the sensitizing concept may not sufficiently differentiate him or her from the layperson's point of view (Huber, 1973, p. 280). In short, this approach does not distinguish the findings of a sociologist from those of the researched subjects.[5] When research interests are guided by the subject, theory, according to Huber, becomes ambiguous and, as a consequence, redundant (Huber, 1973, p. 281).

Huber's views elicited a vigorous rebuttal from Blumer, who, in general, argued that the symbolic interactionist approach does not lack a theory simply because it does not include the "logico-theoretic component" (Blumer, 1973, p. 797). The sensitizing concept is a vehicle for theoretical shaping by an "on-going, flexible, shifting examination of the empirical field" (Blumer, 1973, p. 768). It is this close, shifting examination that holds promise because it is only through such a means that various points of view can be tested.

Whatever methodological ideas Blumer had in the 1930s, they were part of an unfolding understanding of what methodology entailed. "Much of Blumer's methodological writing," states Martyn Hammersley (1989, p.

113), "takes the form of critical assessments on the use of quantitative techniques in sociology, and of the methodological ideas underlying their use." Hammersley (1989, p. 89) claims that in his first works, on the impact of films, Blumer emphasized "the need to capture the attitudes or perspectives which mediate the effects of objective factors." A closer reading of Blumer's approach in 1931 suggests that then, as in 1954, he already advocated the view that concepts should not become divorced from experience, lest they become "indefinite and metaphysical" (Blumer, 1931, p. 531). Already in that 1931 article, Blumer saw concepts, whether scientific or sociological, as "ways of construing certain contents of experience" (1931, p. 518). "Concepts," Blumer declared, "without a perceptual base are indeed insecure" (1931, p. 531).

There are others, however, who feel justified in saying that Blumer's sensitizing concept represents a continuity of his earlier work. Gideon Sjoberg and Roger Nett (1968, p. 59) claim that the use of sensitizing concepts is "consistent with his [Blumer's] image of reality." The individual, accordingly, shapes and reshapes his environment. Even in a bureaucracy that seems to place the individual in an "iron cage," trapped in ossified social institutions, the individual often massages the rules to fit local or interpersonal settings. The social order is not static, but is fluid and endowed with meaning that emerges from its constituent elements.

Characteristically, Blumer elaborated the idea of sensitizing concepts after nearly 20 years of scholarship. Already in his 1931 work, he spoke of the "role of the concept in sensitizing perceptions" (Blumer, 1931, p. 527). He reaffirmed his 1931 position in 1940 when he articulated the idea that social phenomena must be observed on the basis of sensing social relations (Blumer, 1940, p. 715). Blumer's methodological concern for developing suitable concepts thus began in the early 1930s but came into sharper focus in 1947, when he urged "observers to improve their 'intimate familiarity' " (Tucker, 1988, p. 111) as a means to overcome the vagueness in the field of industrial relations.

Just as sensitizing concepts emerge during the gathering of data, the notion of sensitizing concepts emerged after Blumer's long-term engagement with the interactionist perspective. Thus, the "rise" of the sensitizing concept occurred long before Blumer's important reference to it (Blumer, 1954). Its "fall" or "disappearance" after 1956 might have been overstated, especially when we consider the many ways in which the idea of sensitizing concepts has permeated our discipline (as discussed in Chapter 1).

Blumer's approach is grounded in the empirical world, and sensitizing concepts are driven by empirical instances, while at the same time they harvest empirical data for theoretical synthesis. Denzin suggests that gathering data in this conceptually relevant way allows hypotheses to be put to the test (1977, p. 48).[6]

Sensitizing Concepts as Lacking in Social Structural Dimensions

We must also address the issue of whether the sensitizing concept warrants our further support (and use) if it, indeed, encompasses the "larger" social structural dimensions of society. Many (see, e.g., Reynolds, 1990, p. 153) have faulted Blumer's approach for deprecating the social-structural dimensions of societal life. Because sensitizing concepts likely involve noninstitutional forms of behavior (although there are many examples of their application to institutional aspects of society), critics of the sensitizing concept have assumed erroneously that the larger "picture" has no relevance or is not addressed by the sensitizing concept. The larger features of society are, they claim, wholly missing from Blumer's interactionist perspective (Reynolds, 1990, p. 157).[7] "Non-essential and highly problematic" is Sheldon Stryker's vigorous characterization of Blumer's treatment of social organization and social structure (1988, p. 37). Stryker, who seems to leave no room for other answers in his sociology, also found Blumer's key essay, "What Is Wrong With Sociological Theory?" (1954), to be "disabling" with regard to the development of theoretical explanations of social life.

Part of the answer to this criticism lies in recent attempts by symbolic interactionists to reconstruct Blumer when dealing with macrolevel issues. Gary Alan Fine (1990, p. 120) gives some notable examples in which interactionists overlay the macro dimensions of societal life with meaning, interaction, experience, and identity.[8] As Kathleen A. Kalab (1987, p. 83) demonstrates in her research on student vocabularies of motive, excuses are aligned and negotiated in culturally appropriate terms—a clear indication of the importance of the larger societal framework. Goffman's *Interaction Ritual* (1967) is quite explicit in demonstrating the role of history and social context of action.

Blumer minces no words when he responds to his critics, who charge that his individuals are unconstrained by social structure. He defines these charges as "a wild and foolish caricature" of his view (Blumer, 1977, p. 286) and describes the position that claims that Mead rejected the existence of structure in human society as "ridiculous" (1969, p. 75). For Blumer, such matters as social roles and status, relations among institutions, and authority arrangements are important only as they enter "into the process of interpretation and definition out of which joint actions are formed" (Blumer, 1969, p. 75). Blumer was deeply concerned about the problems of the wider society that he had pursued actively since the early 1940s, whether race relations, collective behavior, fashion, or industrial relations (Morrione, 1988, pp. 10-11). David R. Maines (1988, p. 51) also presents a broad range of areas that Blumer has covered in his research and writings, namely stratification, power relations, economic structures, and social change, among others.

The issue of whether Blumer (and, by extension, the sensitizing concept) ever considered the macrosociological perspective becomes more complex when we hear such scholars as Maines claim that it is often symbolic interactionists themselves who have accepted the myth that Blumer did not have a macrosociology (Maines, 1988, p. 43). Maines's treatment of Blumer's nayers and sayers with respect to macrosociology is rather thorough and can be read with much profit, because of his presentation of textual evidence of Blumer's macrosociology. That treatment carries considerable weight in our judgment, as Maines is regarded by many as a "true interactionist." Chapter 5 in this volume demonstrates the use of a sensitizing concept to illustrate and analyze the social organization of science, politics, and fisheries management.

Sensitizing Concepts as
Characterized by Vagueness

As noted earlier, some 20 years after its coinage, scholars such as Joan Huber (1973, p. 280) find fault with sensitizing concepts lacking "specific objective benchmarks." John Lofland, some 8 years earlier, was already wary of the "conceptual impoverishment" that attends to interactionist research in general and to interactionist concepts in particular (Lofland, 1970, p. 38). There is some merit in his critique that qualitative researchers generally have not followed through in their use of concepts, bringing their analysis to theoretical fruition. For that reason, he claims, noninteractionists see such impoverishment as a "license for subjectivism and a relinquishing of proper scientific procedure" (Lofland, 1970, p. 38). We offer "mechanisms, devices, strategies" but, in the end, we have remained "unsystematic" or "elusive" in our conclusions.

These criticisms of symbolic interactionism, and of the sensitizing concept in particular, have persisted. Even as recently as 1990, Kenneth Baugh, Jr., for example, claimed that when Blumer stressed the tentative nature of sensitizing concepts, he did not rid social theory of conceptual vagueness.[9] The vagueness of social scientific concepts simply shifted to the vagueness and ambiguity of sensitizing concepts (Baugh, 1990, p. 30). Blumer's brief mention of sensitizing concepts in a 1977 rebuttal (Blumer, 1977, pp. 285-289) to a critic did not, according to Baugh (1990, p. 32), dispel the difficulties of sensitizing concepts.[10]

Blumer (1954, pp. 8-9) had, however, anticipated some of these objections. First, he admitted that social theorists are likely to reject sensitizing concepts as vague and indefinite; second, they would misconstrue the grounding on sense, rather than on explicit objective traits, as too informal an exposition; and third, they would take the proponents of sensitizing concepts to task for allowing vague stereotypes, rather than progressive refinements, to seize hold of data.[11] Blumer had challenged J. Davis Lewis (1976) when the latter claimed that sensitizing concepts had no objective referents. Unequivocally, Blumer speaks of sensitizing concepts as "observable concrete instances" (Blumer, 1977, p. 286). He exhorted his students and colleagues to "test concepts," because he saw the need for sociologists not to use them unthinkingly, as vague abstractions to be employed in unclear and imprecise ways (Becker, 1988, pp. 14-15; Morrione, 1988, p. 10).[12]

David Wellman (1988) has produced a serious rebuttal to charges that Blumer's sociological method was flawed, vague, and unoperationable. For Denzin (1977, pp. 48-49), the sensitizing approach offers one of the best means of grappling with the distinct features of the empirical world:

> This method demands an intimate familiarity with the empirical world. It dictates a sensitive awareness of negative cases. It forces the judicious collection of illustrative instances that reflect one's concepts. (Denzin, 1977, p. 49)

It seems more likely that the critics of sensitizing concepts may have considered only the initial stages in the development of the sensitizing concept, which, by nature, seems more vague than operational or definitive concepts. As data are collected, the sensitizing concept becomes more clearly rooted in the empirical world. Becker argues strongly that in his conceptual contribution to sociology, Blumer was never "anti-theoretical, anti-empirical, or anti-measurement" (Becker, 1988, p. 14). The sensitizing concept points to something we observe but cannot yet define adequately. Use of the sensitizing concept, however, is much closer to the mark, because "you [know] what you [are] doing" (Becker, 1988, p. 16), unlike the thoughtless invocation of many other concepts in sociology.

It seems important to stress the fact that even when sociologists try to create definite concepts, many still struggle with the sort of ambiguity and vagueness usually associated with sensitizing concepts. Despite their importance, sociological concepts are woefully inexact (Riggs, 1979, pp. 173-175). Mills was wont to refer to definite concepts as "tinfoil" concepts (1959, p. 141). Some, such as Charles Edgley and Ronny E. Turner (1979, p. 193), highlight the notion that creativity, insight, and meaning are more likely to occur when there is, initially, ambiguity.

From all I have said, sensitizing concepts need not be vague, despite the descriptor "sensitizing," which initially would lead one to conclude that such concepts are, indeed, vague. Although the terms "operational" and "definitive" conjure up less vagueness, there is no guarantee that they are actually less vague: Blumer effectively exposed their empty superficiality and lack of specific empirical referents. Mills would, several years later, denounce the "fetishism of the Concept" (Mills, 1959, p. 50).

It is important to stress that sensitizing concepts have a career. The social researcher may adopt a highly provisional concept that he may drop in the early stages of research and that he finds vague for his purposes. Another concept might hold well throughout the course of investigation, and the researcher might decide to keep it for clarity.

Sensitizing Concepts as Nominal Definitions

If the sensitizing concept is to be meaningful as a research tool, it must exhibit the power of explanation that only "real" definitions can offer. H. Warren Dunham (1970, pp. 28-29) underscores the view that, because sensitizing concepts are nominal, such concepts are not definite in character and do not designate specific types of reality. For Dunham, moreover, when using sensitizing concepts, it is "well-nigh impossible to develop a science in the accepted meaning of the term" (Dunham, 1970, p. 29). There is no basis for others, such as Baugh (1990, p. 28), to claim that Blumer has simply engaged in "semantic reductionism."

Nominal definitions are terms used in place of other terms, as opposed to real, definitive, or operational definitions that precisely measure data. As an example, a nominal definition of a vehicle would be "a motorized vehicle," whereas a real definition specifies it as "a carriage supplied with an engine fueled by gasoline." In the former instance, the nominal definition provides us with no relationships, in contrast to the latter, real, definition. Robert Bierstedt (1959, p. 121) favors the use of real definitions because nominal definitions can put closure on research and delimit the ensuing research. He supports Blumer's view that one "needs to rely on the investigation itself to determine whether or not the properties the definition ascribes to the concept actually do belong to it (Bierstedt, 1959, p. 125).[13]

Symbolic interactionists reject the idea that sensitizing concepts are nominal, but how do we come to the rescue of sensitizing concepts that some define as nominal? There is an inherent tension or struggle in our attempts to observe social phenomena. A tension exists because the observer must, at once, try to reconcile social features that are both universal and particular (Baugh, 1990, p. 29). For Blumer, sensitizing concepts are ideal bridges between the universal and the particularity of experience. In disentangling a heated argument between George A. Lundberg and Herbert Blumer, Bierstedt (1959) makes it clear that sensitizing concepts not only are "real" definitions but also are an integral part of theory building. For Bierstedt, the

> [r]eal definitions not only indicate the meaning of the word, . . . but they also assert something about the referent of the concept defined. . . . A real definition . . . can serve as a premise in inference and . . . as an hypothesis concerning the nature of the phenomenon under investigation . . .; it operates both on the referential level and on the symbolic level. (Bierstedt, 1959, p. 130)

Sociologists, according to Bierstedt, are all engaged in the task of making assertions about society, using concepts that have referents in the empirical world. He assures us that their use involves substantive theory and is "the ultimate goal of sociological theory" (Bierstedt, 1959, p. 144).

Chapter 4 offers several steps to ensure that sensitizing concepts remain "real definitions" as one moves forward in constructing them from the perspective of the research participants: the use of focus groups, "inspection," "dimensionalization," metaphor, irony, and the like.

Sensitizing Concepts as Restricting the Range for Collecting Data

According to Sheldon Stryker, "Blumer severely restricts the legitimate range of investigatory (data gathering) techniques as well as analytic methods." Stryker, already not willing to cede anything constructive about Blumer's ideas, finds that *exploration* and *inspection* (which are particular stages in developing a sensitizing concept) represent these sorts of restrictions in particular (1988, pp. 36 and 41, fn. 6). The substance of Stryker's criticism of Blumer's approach is twofold. On one hand, because Blumer argues against the use of a priori theory, deductive hypotheses, and methods that do not center on the actors' interpretations, Stryker thinks that mathematical and statistical data must be ruled out in research involving sensitizing concepts (1988, p. 36). Moreover, Stryker finds little, if any, comfort in the stress Blumer places on participatory observation as the "only" means to collect data (Stryker, 1988, p. 36). Stryker's other criticism is directed against Blumer's belief that the meanings of actors are negotiated, in flux, transitional, and so on. Adopting such an approach, Stryker argues, one is forced to discount the notion that meanings are either historically or social-structurally constituted (1988, p. 37). Such an approach also limits the range of data that can be collected usefully, because neither historical documents nor structural accounts are resorted to by Blumerian researchers.

It might, at first, seem difficult to question the validity of Stryker's arguments. Statistical reasoning is indeed not part of Blumer's approach, although conventional "counting" is a technique usually not ignored in qualitative approaches. Moreover, to argue that historical and structural data are not relied upon is not a fair characterization of the use of sensitizing concepts. Researchers are fully aware that the meanings that actors attach to their world can be both historically and social-structurally derived.

We should speak more forcefully when we say that the approach advocated by Blumer when using sensitizing concepts ensures the collection of a wider range of data: It is not only the researcher's framework that works itself into a research setting; more significantly, the researcher must consider the depth and range of ideas and actions, expressed by the participants in the research, that might shed light on the subject. When we acknowledge the usefulness of the research participants' point of view, our gaze is directed to a greater richness of data than if we had simply relied on ourselves and on our own perspective. What is more relevant is Blumer's idea that, in addition to enabling other researchers to review and examine the field researcher's range and use of data, there is plenty of room for the investigator to choose the questions, the nature, or the range of data (Blumer, 1980, p. 413).

Sensitizing Concepts as Going Stale

When concepts become widely accepted, there is the danger of not recognizing their original limitations. Paul Atkinson (1984, p. 949) suggests that some concepts become so well established that without periodic critical review, they can go stale. As in the case of uncertainty in medical sociology, R. Fox (1957) shows that in her study of the culture of medical students, "training for uncertainty" has become a necessary prerequisite to professional competence. In fact, uncertainty is "also portrayed as an almost essential quality of medical knowledge and practice" (Atkinson, 1984, p. 950). Atkinson, moreover, saw the concept as so appealing that it has taken on a life of its own in the sociological literature on medicine. We now assume that medical training and knowledge is fraught with uncertainty, more so than certainty. The concept has now become so overemphasized that we ignore the limitations of this particular sensitizing concept.

Sensitizing concepts are meant to undergo change (even though there are not many examples of this). C. Wright Mills reminds us that when a concept becomes a fetish, it may outlive specific and empirical problems. Encrusted with old meanings, concepts simply fall to the floor, rather than enabling one to fly high to "see something in the social world more clearly" (Mills, 1959, p. 48). A sympathetic interactionist, Charles Tucker (1988, p. 105), directs our gaze to one of Blumer's earliest works, in which the latter claims that scientific concepts (as opposed to everyday, common-sense ones) "have a career, changing their meaning from time to time in accordance with the introduction of new experiences and replacing one content with another" (Blumer, 1931, p. 524). Blumer envisioned that career as starting with an "initial trial stage" and culminating in a "highly refined" stage (1931, p. 529). All these concerns of Blumer's urge us to see that concepts should ideally have a dynamic lifespan.

Although the purposes of criticisms differ widely (some are castigations, others are benevolent or helpful), it is instructive for the reader to be apprised of them. The preceding discussion of six criticisms, I hope, has been a source of insights about the empirical and theoretical basis of sensitizing concepts. We found that Blumer's insistence on using the sensitizing concept is in full accord with his sociological methods. To those who claim that sensitizing concepts (and, by implication, interactionist thought) do not take into account social structural phenomena, we hope it has been demonstrated that this is not so: They do acknowledge social organization. We also have learned that Blumer had anticipated that the gist of criticisms of sensitizing concepts would be that the concepts are vague, but to coin concepts as "definitive" or "operational" does not make them any clearer or less vague. To accuse those who use sensitizing concepts of restricting the range of data collecting is entirely unjustified (as we have seen, some of the critics are antipathetic to Blumer's approach in any event). Every data collection method is restrictive; the use of sensitizing concepts is no more or less so. There is, however, evidence that without critical examination, sensitizing concepts can go stale.

What is needed now is a clearer formulation of how sensitizing concepts are created, applied, and related to theory. The following chapters address these concerns.

NOTES

1. Morrione (1988, p. 2) offers a sampling of Blumer's antagonists.

2. Blumer (1980, p. 411) highlights the fact that Mead "did not deal in his writings or his lectures with the methodological problems involved in applying his scheme to the study of human conduct and human group life."

3. Baugh (1990, p. 31) highlights the drawbacks of Blumer's sensitizing concepts by claiming that these concepts represent an anomaly in Blumer's social thought. Citing Blumer's 1931 paper, Baugh found that Blumer had spoken out against concepts that were treated in a "loose, common sense" manner.

4. There is an extensive literature concerning whether Blumer's sociology ("symbolic interactionism") represents Mead's theoretical and methodological perspective (see, e.g., Blumer, 1980, and Huber, 1973).

5. For Huber (1973, p. 280), this problem remains even when one decides to adopt the perspective of the underdog, as Becker (1970) suggests.

6. As Noel Iverson suggests, this approach may or may not be relevant, depending on one's research interest and the kinds of theoretical questions one puts to the "world" (personal communication, October 8, 1995).

7. Structural functionalists leveled a similar critique against Max Weber's ideal types (Martindale, 1959, pp. 82-83).

8. The eagerness to embrace macro societal dimensions has led interactionists to be "almost promiscuous in their willingness to thrash in any theoretical bedding" (Fine, 1990, p. 120).

9. Becker claims that Blumer's primary contribution to sociological theory was conceptual (Becker, 1988).

10. I disagree with Baugh (1990, p. 30) when he states that Blumer, in the 1977 rebuttal, made a "noncommittal" mention of sensitizing concepts. The relevant article, which aroused such a strong reaction on the part of Blumer, held 16 "inaccurate characterizations" (Blumer, 1977, p. 286), and Blumer selected four of the most important ones for rebuttal. Sensitizing concepts constituted one of them.

11. A positivist and a pragmatist would argue that vagueness arises when a concept is not grounded in reality. Such "grounding" must be anchored to two kinds of variables, antecedents and consequences (Paul McDonnell, personal communication, October 6, 1995).

12. Shibutani (1988, p. 29) is emphatic in his claim that Blumer "did not seem to realize that empirically grounded hypotheses are testable but that concepts are not." Shibutani, moreover, was not able to deduce from Blumer's writing what precisely Blumer had in mind with "testing" concepts.

13. Blumer himself showed no, or at least little, interest in whether concepts are nominal or real, and he has found the literature in this area "dull and of slight value" (1931, p. 517).

3. TAKING DISTANCE FROM THE DATA

What scares many research novices (and longtime practitioners!) is, to put it plainly, what to do with the collected data and how those data get written up. How do we translate, interpret, or carry our data into our writing and analysis? One usually feels quite at home and even looks forward to learning new data-gathering techniques; it is the writing and analysis of data that seems so formidable at times. Part of the answer lies in acknowledging that writing and analysis do not usually follow data gathering. All these processes often occur simultaneously. The use of sensitizing concepts makes good sense because it keeps our feet in both the data gathering and analytical stages, which in both theory and practice should not, or cannot, be separated.

This chapter suggests that sensitizing concepts can be likened to halfway houses where data are temporarily stored and made ready for analysis. It compares several such halfway houses, namely everyday (or "folk") concepts, sensitizing concepts, and sensitizing supra-concepts. The process of distancing oneself from the data implies the ever-larger encapsulation of empirical data that not only allows one to link micro and macro levels of social organization but also puts data into perspective. This process is necessary to adopt a theoretical or analytical framework. Martyn Hammersley and Paul Atkinson (1983, p. 180) offer the advice that sensitizing concepts "are an important starting point . . . the germ of the emerging theory." One could argue that without the intrinsic process of distancing, sensitizing concepts are fruitless.

We can find the seedbed of sensitizing concepts in some of the most significant works that have given shape to sociology. Many readers are familiar with Simmel's *social forms*, which represent a derivation of "elements from the raw stuff of experience," shaping them "into determinate unities" (Levine, 1971, p. xiv). Social forms have their origins in the empirical world and in social experience, but in the metaphorical sense, they acquire an existence of their own. From the other side of the coin, sensitizing concepts originate in the particular empirical world but must acquire an objective form of their own for the purpose of generating analysis and theory. Very much like the subject's ordinary understanding of the social world, the protocol of the researcher's world cannot fully be distinguished from that of the social world in which the researcher finds herself (Emmet & MacIntyre, 1970, p. 1).

All such concepts take progressive distance from the data. To "take distance" from the data is to speak metaphorically. We commonly use sensitizing concepts more than we realize. In everyday life, we constantly cast the experiences and expressions of others—and of ourselves—in some generalizing manner. Following Alfred Schutz, our identification of experience is based on familiar "sensory observations in general and of the experience of overt action in particular," all of which "excludes several dimensions of social reality from all possible enquiry" (Schutz, 1970, p. 7). Schutz speaks of the social basis of knowledge as an outcome of this generalizing process. In the normal course of experiencing society, we already work with abstract conceptualizations of others' actions or thoughts. We order our experience and the experience of others into categories. In our efforts to interpret the behavior of others, we resort to abstractions. These abstractions involve a degree of taking distance from the social world. We can understand the verbal and nonverbal cues only if we have vessels to cast them into, a *vocabulary of motives* such as in accounts for skipping class (Kalab, 1987).[1] The very existence of language allows us to form concepts. Kenneth Hoover and Todd Donovan (1995, p. 18) aver that language itself is "nothing more than huge collections of names for things, feelings, and ideas generated . . . by people in the course of relating to each other and to their environment."

Whether we acknowledge it or not, we know that all data, including those that are the closest to the subject's world, are already abstracted knowledge, or theory, albeit less systematic and rigorous than the observer's (Hammersley, 1985, p. 246). Charles Tucker makes a strong point when he refers to Blumer's sentiment that through the unique ability of human beings to conceptualize the empirical world, they can not only reorganize that world but also transcend it (Tucker, 1988, p. 104).

I would now like to explore more specifically the three groups of concepts that progressively take distance from the data. Closest to the data, one finds folk concepts. Concepts that are, metaphorically speaking, the most distant from the data are within the family of terms. Straddling folk terms, on one hand, and the family of terms, on the other, are sensitizing concepts. I include a number of specific examples of concepts in each group, both to underscore the more general points being made and to develop an appreciation for the diverse and insightful concepts that sociologists have developed over the years.

Folk Concepts or Terms

The group of concepts closest to the data consists of folk terms (Goffman, 1967, p. 129), which occupy an important place in the symbolic interactionist approach to understanding everyday life. John Lofland (1970) speaks of these as "mini-concepts" that, in his view, are usually not elaborated upon to the extent to which they deserve. Following this line of thought, Norman K. Denzin urges us to maintain a distinction between "first-order" and "second-order" constructs (Denzin, 1989, p. 9; see also Emmet & MacIntyre, 1970). He sees the former as the language of everyday life and the latter as expressing abstract and sociological language. Similarly, anthropologists such as Clifford Geertz in *Local Knowledge* (1983) are now using the equivalent of sensitizing concepts when they use "experience-near" concepts, which

> someone—a patient, a subject, in our case an informant—might himself naturally and effortlessly use to define what he or his fellows see, feel, think, imagine, and so on. (Geertz, 1983, p. 57)

Hammersley and Atkinson (1983, p. 130) draw our attention to Mills's use of "situated vocabularies" leading to "potential lines of inquiry." For Diesing, they are "concrete concepts" that are used by people to organize and interpret their experience, to construct their own world and give meaning to it" (Diesing, 1971, p. 209). Glaser and Strauss are happy with the use of "local" concepts in identifying a "few principal or gross features" of the social setting (1967, p. 45). It is these concepts that participant-observers must learn if they wish to enter and understand the subculture of their research subjects. For Schutz (1962, p. 62), they are "constructs of the first level," or commonsense constructs, whereby we gain an actor's subjective understanding of his or her action, "negative action" (i.e., nonaction), or setting.

The social landscape is filled with stereotypes that are everyone's creations. Just as sociologists can be "meaning-readers" (Nettler, 1970, pp. 54-55), individuals also employ understandings in their explanations of the behavior of others. When one "engages in the search for the meanings of acts [of others], he looks for beliefs, definitions, and attitudes." Others call upon a "symbolic repertoire" (Nettler, 1970, p. 56) that can explain the others' attitudes or behavior toward the subjects. What makes the examination of such stereotypes challenging is the fact that they sometimes represent very hardened social attitudes. Indeed, as Hammersley and Atkinson (1983, p. 131) point out, the "most banal . . . fiction is often replete with images, stereotypes, and myths." Such fiction is filled with conventional wisdom or stupidity, a commonsensical view, dealing with such "cultural themes" as "sex, gender, family, work, success, failure" and so on (Hammersley & Atkinson, 1983, p. 131). Although usually express-ing prejudice and ignorance, such fiction cannot be ignored by the social scientist who must take the stereotypes into consideration when attempting to understand the others' construction of the subjects' experience. John and Lyn Lofland (1995, p. 106) remind us of Orrin Klapp's work (1958) on the matter of "coding" people, which Klapp refers to as *social typing*. Social types arise out of the merging of what constitutes individual and idiosyn-cratic behavior on one hand, and formal or informal role behavior on the other (Lofland & Lofland, 1995, p. 106). The list of conceptual candidates for social typing is endless, as they are steeped in stereotypical attitudes.

The existence of these vessels allows us to generalize such cues and make them understandable in a common, everyday manner. They are like folk terms or concepts into which we pour observable data. Let us take some everyday illustrations (which were found through research). The men in Roethlisberger's well-known study of the Bank-Wiring Room at the Hawthorne Electric plant in Cicero, Chicago, "held certain definite ideas as to the way in which an individual should conduct himself." Overeager workers were "ratebusters," those who performed too little work were "chisellers," and those who reported to a supervisor to the detriment of the group were "squealers" (Roethlisberger & Dickson, 1961, p. 522). Such terms invite other workers both consciously and unconsciously to identify a variety of attributes that define zealous, lazy, or spying workers. Our social world is filled with similar stereotypes and labels—all folk concepts. In a sense, we are speaking of a *definition of the situation* that shapes our attitudes and behaviors to conform to what we think is expected of us.

Let us take another example from everyday life. We can use the concept of hope to provide a convenient place to store a wide variety of observable data, which also vary from person to person, or from culture to culture. Hope can express "fortitude" in the presence of adversity or a last-ditch effort (as in "let's hope for the best"). The vocabulary of hope also implies "encouragement," or the idea of "never give up hope." There are still other definitions: a medical doctor's giving someone hope of recovery from illness may well mean that, in fact, there is no remedy in sight. A school principal stating that she "hopes that you will do better" can imply a reward or threat. When incumbents share a particular world of meaning, variances will be only slight; the less such worlds are shared, the more likely it is that people will disagree on the meaning of folk concepts.

At times, someone's world of meaning engulfs another person's. In other words, the bulk of everyday interactions is filled with people's construc-tions of someone else's experience. Linda Turner, a graduate student who lives in an area characterized by high unemployment and people on welfare, noticed that government officials and those "on the dole"[2] have the habit of using the stereotype "social junk" to refer to those on welfare (Turner, 1994). Even when such terms originate outside the group, the minority may accept the label assigned to it by the more powerful majority. "Social junk" is a strong indicator of a group's social status and its relationship to the larger society.

Not all stereotypes are negative: Many are positive in orientation. A curiously interesting example of such stereotyping is the term "eccentric," which blends both positive and negative meanings, although overwhelmingly the former. The media often consider musicians, such as the late Janis Joplin, as eccentric. The film *Amadeus* portrays Mozart as an eccentric. Society[3] cherishes eccentrics: No one understands what they are up to, but they have the characteristic of being harmless and even leading fruitful lives that benefit society. These typifications (Lofland & Lofland, 1984, p. 74) are common enough to warrant attention by the social researcher, so that they can be incorporated as useful sensitizing concepts. The typifications convey deeply held commonsense opinions that must be understood by the researcher.

There is a drawback in only using folk terms: They may lack the precision necessary for a detailed understanding of the social phenomenon (Hoover & Donovan, 1995, p. 19). Such terms, as Hammersley and Atkinson (1983, p. 178) argue, arise "spontaneously" from the research participants' world of beliefs and behavior. Although it is important to recognize the value of such spontaneous emergence of terms, we need some help in moving these terms closer to an analytic framework. This is where we need sensitizing concepts that are formally defined by the social scientist. Faced with the challenge of incorporating useful and evocative folk terms in their research, some sociologists claim that sensitizing concepts should reflect a "natural attitude" toward everyday life common to both laypeople and sociologists (Heap & Roth, 1973, p. 363). In a sense, sociologists or anthropologists are tempted to skim the empirical surface in their efforts to denote sensitizing concepts.

Sensitizing Concepts

When folk terms become "located within more general analytic frameworks" (Hammersley & Atkinson, 1983, p. 178), we speak of them as sensitizing concepts. Sensitizing concepts in sociological literature share the characteristics of folk concepts in the way they articulate generalizable knowledge. Whereas folk concepts are roughly equivalent to an actor's definition of the situation, sensitizing concepts are the sociologist's definition of the definition of the situation: the definition of the situation's definition.

The difference between the everyday use of folk concepts and sociological sensitizing concepts is that sensitizing concepts are constructed for analytical purposes. Folk concepts are highly concrete or very vague and easily stretched, whereas sensitizing concepts try to be more abstract and less context-dependent. As a consequence, sensitizing concepts have more generality and thus more theoretical utility. For Denzin (1989, p. 12), the social scientist must continually attempt to "lift one's own idiosyncratic experience to the level of the consensual and shared meanings." The more skeptical users of sensitizing concepts would claim that sensitizing concepts are no more than "constructs of constructs" of the everyday world by everyday people (Hindess, 1972, p. 2). Schutz calls them "scientific constructs on the second level," which, nevertheless, must include a reference to the "subjective meaning an action has for the actor" (1962, p. 62). For Diesing (1971), it is not merely a matter of amplifying an actor's folk term but more a question of making it more applicable to a wider set of actors. He claims that sensitizing concepts do not derive from the culture of a single community. The thrust of his argument is similar to mine, namely that sensitizing concepts are the key to developing a general or analytic framework:

> [Sensitizing concepts] are developed in the comparison of cases by finding similar or common elements among them all. They refer to the general rather than the unique and thus make cross-cultural understanding possible. (Diesing, 1971, p. 209)[4]

In what way are sensitizing concepts different from folk terms? First, sociologists strive for a conscious use of the term. Such use implies a deliberate attempt to move not only some distance from the everyday world but also a distance from one's own subjective view of the world. We can imagine a sensitizing concept as a neutral ground where the concepts and language of the social world and those of the researcher meet. A sensitizing concept preferably retains the word usage of the research subject, allowing us to keep roots in the empirical world; however, a researcher retains such terms for evocative purposes. Robert Bogdan (1988), for example, retains the term "freak show" when he talks about people presenting human oddities for amusement and profit. Laud Humphreys (1970) uses "tearoom trade" in reference to his work on homosexuality in public washrooms. Meg Luxton (1980) makes effective use of women's housework as a "labour of love" by its elaboration into *More Than a Labour of Love* as the title of her study.

Kathy Charmaz is a gifted sociologist who manages to incorporate folk terms as sensitizing concepts. She takes a close look in her 1990 paper at the interactions between the chronically ill and their family members. As the ill increasingly run out of stamina, strength, or even purpose, they describe the importance of their family's "being there." This sensitizing concept effectively directs our gaze at the importance of the presence of family members and their value in the efforts of the chronically ill to retain some semblance of normality.

Second, sensitizing concepts enable us to frame the studied activity as a social process. For example, we can well imagine how such coined terms as "aces, keeners, sucks, browners," and "dumb dumbs" (Albas & Albas, 1994, p. 274) in Daniel and Cheryl Albas's study of student culture are derived from the labelers' perspective, setting into motion self-defining processes. "Keeping one's nose to the grindstone in the same study is also a sensitizing concept, because it catches the social processes of work discipline and a studious avoidance of distractions (Albas & Albas, 1994, p. 278). John Lofland's own dictum, however, suggests that sociologists generally treat concepts with too little care. Thus, findings are "sadly lacking in what one might call 'mini-concepts' " (Lofland, 1970, p. 37). It is therefore important to create a set of "limited and precise notions of microscopic social processes" (Lofland, 1970, p. 37).

Erving Goffman (1986, pp. 146-147) offers an excellent example of such "mini-concepts" when he uses "stigma," wherein subjects construct some meaning about their own experience and organize their attitudes and behaviors around that meaning. Once stigmatized, or under the threat or fear of being stigmatized, individuals employ coping mechanisms that they believe will deal with physical, documentary (a "prison record"), or contextual ("bad company") facets of their lives (Mann, 1983, p. 378). Individuals will handle the stigma, whether actual or only potential, by highlighting its presence or by hiding it altogether. Harold Garfinkle's (1956) concept of "status degradation ceremonies" is another good example of a term coined by the researcher that is eminently precise and yet faithful to the empirical world. Status degradation ceremonies characterize a set of "[c]ommunicative work[s] directed to transforming an individual's identity into an identity lower in the group's scheme of social types" (Garfinkle, 1956, p. 420).

Third, a sensitizing concept serves to construct an analytic framework. People commonly use folk concepts to express a particular worldview, but the sociologist strives to put in place a concept that serves as a halfway house for gathering data, in anticipation of some theoretical insight. Blumer speaks of sensitizing concepts as the "gateway" to the world of theory (1954, p. 9). Used in this way, sensitizing concepts are "holding pens" for data conveniently grouped around an image, one usually created by the research participants. Robert Stebbins, for example, in his study of comedians on stage, uses the definition of art to organize his knowledge about what it takes to be a stand-up comedian: learning the art, acquiring material, organizing an act, and performing the act (1994, pp. 258-259). Having his data thus arranged, Stebbins then considers three kinds of artistic skills that are called for, namely making or doing something for an aesthetic experience; expressing or communicating past experiences; and designing, composing, and performing through personal interpretation. Charged with knowledge derived from gathering data about stand-up comedians, researchers can then look at other forms of artistic expression.

The concept of "master status" (Hughes, 1945) expresses a researcher's construction of a phenomenon that involves both the subject and the other.[5] As members of the human community, we carry in our hearts and minds expectations of social traits associated with particular social positions. It is through the work of the media, cartoons, films, and ordinary talk, Everett C. Hughes reminds us, that such expectations become as fixed as concrete (1945, p. 355). When these expectations contradict uncharacteristic status positions, we have the notion of master status (Hughes, 1945, p. 357), such as in the case of a horseback rider who is physically handicapped. An example from the late twentieth century can be found in one of Marge Piercy's novels, *The Longings of Women* (1994), in which one of the main characters, Mary Burke, is a housecleaner but is also homeless. Coming out of a divorce, she has lost everything—her stylish middle-class home, her golf club privileges, even her family photo albums. Reduced to living on the streets of Boston, she manages to stay in homes she cleans when the occupants are away. She carries her good clothes in her handbag and she wears them when she enters these homes. She keeps her two statuses strictly separate and is prudent in doing so: Once the cleaning agency finds out she lives on the streets, she loses her livelihood (still not enough for even a rental deposit for a modest apartment) and is fired. Everything else becomes meaningless if she becomes visible as a homeless person. Being homeless is the master status, overshadowing all her other statuses: paid housecleaner, a parent to adult children (she even hides her homeless status from her grown-up children), and so on.

Fourth, sensitizing concepts allow one to undertake the necessary work of the "constant comparative method" (a term coined by Glaser and Strauss, 1967). As it is quite impossible to apply small bits of data in one social setting to another setting, it is important to create vessels large enough to hold vast amounts of empirical data. These vessels allow us to conceptualize broader empirical situations in which to make comparisons. The marriage of sensitizing concepts to the constant comparative method allows one to generalize, indeed, to transfer, findings to other social settings. By constantly comparing the data across these various settings, we contribute to a theoretical framework. The constant comparative method creates sensitizing concepts out of folk terms and lifts these concepts to a higher level of empirical and theoretical relevance. Robert E. Edgerton, for example, looks at ways in which persons with mental retardation.[6] Employing the concept of the management of stigma, he concludes that such persons are eloquent and plaintive in their determination to raise their self-esteem. The management of stigma should be seen in the context of the need by human beings, including those with mental retardation, to make self-esteem a primary goal of their thoughts and actions.

For its simplicity and yet its highly effective ability to be used in the study of other social settings, I particularly like Arlie Hochschild's term, "emotion work." Emotion work (1983, p. 19) refers to the act of managing one's emotions according to the requirements of company manuals, so that one's private ways are transmuted into something that can be displayed and sold as labor. Whether a person works as an airline attendant, a Wal-Mart greeter, a door-to-door salesperson (whether selling religion or vacuum cleaners), or a professor in front of a class, he or she must manage "feeling rules," whether this means magnifying and sustaining feelings or curbing them. Hochschild's concern is that what "we do privately, often unconsciously, to feelings . . . nowadays often falls under the sway of large organizations, social engineering, and the profit motive" (Hochschild, 1983, p. 19). The important point is that I can use such concepts as emotion work or feeling rules when looking at other settings. When I am able to apply concepts in a research setting other than the original one, I find that my enthusiasm for sociology is rekindled.

Fifth, sensitizing concepts proceed along with the data rather than from some ideas that existed before collecting data. We all step into the world of data with preconceived ideas, but by allowing the development of a concept close to the data, we can be more certain that the sensitizing concept occupies, as stated earlier, a neutral ground. Blumer (1977) insists that sensitizing concepts must proceed from concrete data, establishing "benchmarks." Karen Hutton (a graduate student at the Department of Sociology at the University of New Brunswick who owns horses) stresses the need to avoid definitive concepts (as Blumer suggests), because they can

> be likened to the blinders placed on the horse. The obscuring of the animal's vision ensures that it will plod straight ahead and not be distracted by any of the interesting, threatening, or startling activities that may be occurring on all sides of his straight and narrow path. (Hutton, 1994)

In this connection, I find it helpful to conceptualize the study of everyday life, for example, in terms of six social processes that can be briefly summarized as: (a) getting involved, (b) acquiring perspectives, (c) achieving identity, (d) doing activity, (e) experiencing relationships, and (f) becoming an "ex."[7] One sets out this general conceptual approach, collecting data accordingly, and goes about refining and reshaping the concepts as one moves forward in the research. Mary Lorenz Dietz's study (1994) of the world of ballet illustrates the manner in which initial assumptions in the gathering of data must make way for new theoretical insights gained along the way. Her initial framework speaks to the importance of parental involvement in the early stages of recruitment in ballet, but she realized, after the collection of data, that "self-criticism" plays an equally, if not more, significant role in recruitment retention of novices—a process that ballet teachers, choreographers, peers, and critics subscribe to in a "closed, competitive," and "total institution-like" environment (1994, p. 67).

Sixth, sensitizing concepts, unlike commonsense concepts, are always the "focus of analysis and always treated as tentative" (Tucker, 1988, p. 104). Barry Hindess (1972, p. 2) sees them as "constructs of the constructs formed in common sense thinking by the actors on the social scene." Although both commonsense and social-scientific concepts can be relatively enduring and unchanging, scientific concepts are more likely to "strain toward consistency" (Blumer, cited by Tucker, 1988, p. 105). Some readers might be already familiar with R. Dubin's (1992) concept of "central life interests," which may well have a long shelf life, analytically speaking, because of its solidity. The concept conveys how subjects see themselves when they make such statements as, "This is who I am," pouring much of their energy, time, and resources into their particular life interest. The absorption is total, involving their physical, intellectual, and emotional energy. "Among all the thousands of choices each person faces in daily life," Dubin states, "the most personal is choosing and living a central life interest" (1992, p. 13).

As we have seen, both folk and sensitizing concepts involve distancing from the data. In a metaphorical sense, the latter type of concepts is more removed from the social world than the former. Moreover, when we discover that some concepts can be applied across diverse settings, we know that we are at the threshold of gaining fresh insights about social processes. When we also find a diverse set of empirical data, we may consider looking for a concept that captures these data. For our purposes, we can call these sensitizing *supra*-concepts. The particular label we assign to this category of sensitizing concepts is not very important; the recognition that such a larger vessel may exist for our analysis is more significant.

Sensitizing Supra-Concepts

The term "sensitizing supra-concepts" refers to that class of concepts that encompasses a wider body of empirical data. A good example of such a concept is "social world" (Unruh, 1983), which is

> an extremely large, highly permeable, amorphous, and spatially transcendent form of social organization wherein actors are linked cognitively through shared perspectives arising out of common channels of communication. (Unruh, 1983, p. 14)

The boundaries of a social world cross over into many kinds of geographical areas but are, nevertheless, integrated through communication, shared activities, and norms.

I offer a second term, "total institution," coined by Erving Goffman (1961) and denoting how institutions encompass one's total character,

> symbolized by the barrier to social intercourse with the outside and to departure that is often built right into the physical plant, such as locked doors, high walls, barbed wire . . . (p. 4)

The above terms transcend more than one setting where human interaction takes place. The concepts of social world and total institution consider the macrolevel dimensions of interaction, involving a large number of people and shaping the ideologies and worldview of their inhabitants.

A third term, "community," is another supra-concept that can cover a broad spectrum of empirical instances. Whereas "social world" involves relations that extend beyond one's community and, indeed, involve several communities, "community" traditionally was contiguously defined as a

A Schema showing concepts' taking distance from the empirical world

Empirical world   *Abstract/theoretical world*

< -- >

Colloquial expressions	Dimensionalizing	Same family of terms
Folk terms (Denzin)	(Glaser & Strauss)	(Goffman)
1st-level constructs (Schutz)	2nd-order concepts	Ideal type
Mini-concepts (J.Lofland)	(Denzin)	(Weber)
1st-order concepts (Denzin)		2nd-level constructs
Experience-near concepts (Geertz)		(Schutz)
Situated vocabularies (Mills)		Experience-distant concepts
Concrete concepts (Diesing)		(Geertz)
Definition of the situation		

Figure 3.1. A schema showing concepts' taking distance from the empirical world

geographical bound "settlement," taking on a corporate life. When, however, we define "community" only in terms of its social, rather than territorial, life, we run into problems. Goffman, for example, has already alluded to the unsatisfactory use of the term "deviant community" (1986, p. 143). Thus, defining a community in terms of only its social relations can be ambiguous: a one-sexed army post, for example, is a deviant community in the sense of its structural makeup but is not a community of deviants (Goffman, 1986, p. 143). Conrad Arensberg and Solon Kimball convey the meaning of community as a "master system encompassing social forms and cultural behavior in interdependent . . . institutions" (1965, p. 3). The term "community," then, can be used in many different ways, whether symbolically, territorially, or in some other sense.

George H. Mead's "conversation of gestures" (1934/1962) is another sensitizing concept that takes in a wide variety of empirical instances. The term refers to the "body language" that is intended to convey a communication or a "conversation," in the form of a wink, a frown, or the like—an "attitude of the body which leads to the [desired] response" in the other (Mead, 1934/1962, pp. 13-14).

We already have noted that we use sensitizing concepts along a continuum, which progressively distances us from the data. Some concepts are so close to the research participant's experience that we call these folk terms; other concepts are so far removed from the research participant's natural social world that they are virtually "owned" by the researcher. Figure 3.1 represents such a continuum, but I have added other terms that the reader has become acquainted with in this chapter and that revolve around the sensitizing concept.

A sensitizing concept involves the following features in the study of the social world. Although born in the social world of research participants, it can acquire a life of its own to permit important insights about social processes in general. The concept shifts between the particular world of the research participants and the universal linkage that characterizes theory building. A good sensitizing concept can become something more abstract and less contextualized than if it were to remain completely in the subjects' social world.

This chapter has explored the relationship of sensitizing concepts to other concepts and terms used to describe human experience. Figuratively speaking, sensitizing concepts are found between "experience-near" and "experience-distant" concepts. In practice, sensitizing concepts may also fall at either end of this continuum. Thus, some sensitizing concepts are successful in maintaining the "experience-near" idea, whereas others can be quite abstract, moving the observed empirical data into a larger halfway house. There is, moreover, considerable variation among sensitizing concepts themselves; they may involve the construction of meaning by the research participant, by others, or by the social researcher. These constructions can be directed not only toward the self but also toward the other. What is left out of this configuration is what subjects say and think about social researchers. The relationships and attitudes of the former toward researchers can be quite evocative!

Having elaborated on the nature of sensitizing concepts, I now turn to the next chapter, where I offer a few suggestions as to how we can go about constructing them.

NOTES

1. I am indebted to Robert Stebbins for citing Kalab's research (Stebbins, 1990, pp. 69-72).

2. In Canada, the "recipients" of unemployment insurance payouts are also known as "UIC claimants," with "UIC" standing for "Unemployment Insurance of Canada."

3. Examining how some societies are more successful than others in fostering eccentric behavior can be a worthwhile research endeavor for someone looking at historical and social forces that shape societies.

4. I refer the reader to Chapter 6, which closely compares ideal types and sensitizing concepts.

5. "Master status" might not be the term we would choose today, perhaps favoring instead such terms as "dominant status," "overshadowing status," or "primary status."

6. Edgerton's (1967) study dealt with persons released from a mental institution.

7. The reader should turn to the work of Mary L. Dietz, Robert Prus, and William Shaffir (1994), which promotes this particular conceptual approach, underscored by several fine articles used in this edited work. I usually encourage graduate students to adopt this initial conceptual approach as a means of helping them organize their data and orientation.

4. CONSTRUCTING SENSITIZING CONCEPTS

There are many different styles of learning a new technique or an unfamiliar body of knowledge. My good friend, Dan Jordan, once told me that humans had at least 40 different ways of learning something new. He had devoted his life as a musicologist, an educator, and an anthropologist to the study of these ways of learning.[1] Although it is not important for us to know either the precise numbers of ways of learning or the nature of those ways, it is relevant to acknowledge the presence of these many paths of knowing. This chapter will speak particularly to those who feel more at home with a step-by-step approach to acquiring new habits of knowing and doing and, in this case, developing sensitizing concepts.

The first step is creating concepts that are formulated by the subjects themselves. Such a "halfway house" stores empirical findings in a manner that is most natural to the research participants. Blumer calls the second step exploration, and in it he advocates the use of focus groups (1969, pp. 40-47; 1980, p. 412). As a third step, it will also be important to "inspect" and "dimensionalize" the concept. Fourth, we must endeavor to construct a sensitizing concept in such a way that we can relate it to other social contexts. Fifth, we must create a "family of terms." For the convenience of readers, I have added some helpful hints that can flesh out the above-mentioned steps.

Developing suitable sensitizing concepts can be a challenging exercise. On one hand, we must come as close as possible to the subject's world; on the other hand, we must generate concepts in such a way that they allow us to have significant insights and draw theoretical linkages about social processes. As discussed earlier, sensitizing concepts provide the link between the particular and the universal. It is the tension between the two that produces some remarkably insightful concepts. Some concepts retain the essential character of the subject's world, whereas others undergo a transformation as they seek higher connections to other concepts.

We are initially presented with a tactical dilemma. If, as Karen Hutton (1994) claims, developing sensitizing concepts involves a "largely intuitive process that arises from the particulars of the self-other interaction," it might be inadvisable to suggest specific steps on how to go about constructing them. This impression is heightened when one considers that Blumer left us with very little guidance on the matter of how to go about constructing sensitizing concepts (Hammersley, 1989, p. 192). For that matter, as Roger Sanjek reminds us (1990, p. 385), the processes by which fieldnotes in the field of anthropology are translated into analysis are given short shrift in the literature of that field.

Many of Blumer's students were well aware of the difficulty in figuring out how to do research following Blumer's guidance (see, e.g., Becker, 1988, p. 19): images of paralysis, long periods of gestation, and a fleeting thesis on the horizon were (and still are) the characteristics associated with developing and testing sensitizing concepts. In my experience, it is difficult for research novices in their initial stages of qualitative research to have faith that a body of data will yield concepts that will capture the subject's world, let alone concepts that lead to theoretical insights.

Blumer insisted that for concepts to be empirically and theoretically useful, they cannot, or must not, be vague. Moreover, he seemed to provide three simple rules (Blumer, 1954, pp. 6-7):

1. One must be clear as to the empirical content of the concept. To what does the concept empirically refer?
2. The concept must have a specific understanding, not a general one. In what way does a concept rise above its commonsensical approach?
3. The finding must be "shown to have a relevant place in the empirical world." How can a specific concept transcend its limited circumstances and be made relevant to the empirical as a whole?

It is this constant testing of the empirical worth of the concept that would make a sensitizing concept a valuable stepping stone to building theory. Blumer, apparently, enjoyed asking colleagues to "test the concept" of x (Morrione, 1988, p. 5): How do people use the concept of x in everyday life? Are there types? Are there genetic features of x? What is the relation of x to an act, to a collective act, or to another x? What is the manner in which x changes or persists? Having established the wider empirical relevance of a concept, we can then take the concept further and make theoretical claims about the studied phenomenon.

Step 1: Deriving Concepts
From Participants' Perspective

The empirical world has, as Blumer points out, an "obdurate character" (Blumer, 1969, pp. 26-27) filled with *meaningful* action. To apply sensitizing concepts successfully, we must not bypass the meaning of the things toward which people act. To bypass such meaning is a "grievous neglect of the role of meaning in the formation of behavior" (Blumer, 1969, p. 3). We must exercise judgment, but it must be based on "sensing the social relations of the situation" (Blumer, 1940, p. 715). Here are some of the steps that take the participant's perspective into account.

Embarking on what an anthropologist calls "indexing" (Sanjek, 1990, p. 386), a sociologist "codes" as a means of sorting out data gathered in fieldnotes and interview transcripts. Coding involves "the discovery and naming of categories," whereby the researcher carefully goes over his or her interview transcripts, fieldnotes, and the like to "produce concepts that seem to fit the data" (Strauss, 1987, pp. 27, 28). This is a time-consuming task but nevertheless an important one, wherein the researcher tries to identify particular phrases that occur repeatedly. It is advisable to invite a colleague, such as a student friend or someone else, to sit down and also make an attempt at coding expressions or phrases that are identified with what people say or do.

The craft of giving the sensitizing concept a name must, insofar as possible, contain a verb or, at least, allow us to imagine placing a verb in the term. This is particularly important when one considers that the immediate and long-range purpose of sensitizing concepts is to capture social processes. Kathy Charmaz, in her book *Good Days, Bad Days*, which concerns chronic illness, the self, and time, uses the term "experiencing elusive time" to refer to ill people as they gradually get used to vague symptoms (1991, pp. 29-30). The chronically ill experience the passage of time in a muted fashion. Their slow progression into illness and their lack of awareness of the erosion of time when doing chores comes to an end when a crisis changes the perception of their chronic illness and the passage of time. The skilled researcher comes as close as he possibly can to the empirical world—skimming the empirical surface—and uses the participants' everyday terms, raising them to the level of sensitizing concepts. For Emmet and MacIntyre, if "the social sciences aim indeed at explaining social reality" (1970, p. 15), second-level concepts must include a reference to the subjective meanings of the actor.

Invariably, sensitizing concepts must be derived from the worldview of the participants and grounded in their perceptions of their experiences. Michael H. Agar (1980, p. 104), in discussing ways of developing categories from interview transcripts, speaks of allowing "categories to grow from the way the informants talked during the interview." We must "take the role of the actor and see his world from that standpoint" (Blumer, 1969, p. 73). Anthropologists call this an *emic* approach, originally coined by the linguist Kenneth Pike, to represent "the way in which members of a society chop up their universe into its various domains (Clifton, 1968, p. 307).[2] After all, they are about how people organize their experience. For qualitative researchers, including anthropologists who favor the emic approach, it is of considerable importance to allow the subject's meanings to be attached to a conceptual framework (Denzin, 1989, p. 14). I would think that using the natural language of our research participants would go a long way to obviate the "sociologese" that many have complained about (e.g., Edgley & Turner, 1979, p. 193), to restore more intelligible insights about the human condition, and to make them more easily available to a wider audience. The less artificial the terms, the more viable they become.

Step 2: "Exploring" and Using Focus Groups

As our line of inquiry becomes increasingly clear, exploration becomes an integral part of developing sensitizing concepts:

> Exploration is by definition a flexible procedure in which the scholar shifts from one to another line of enquiry, adopts new points of observation as his study progresses, moves in new directions previously unthought of, and changes his recognition of what are relevant data as he acquires more information and better understanding. (Blumer, 1969, p. 40)

As Blumer (1980, p. 412) sees it, sociologists use *exploration* for studies of groups with which they have no intimate familiarity or when they are struggling with empirical data. The principal aim of exploration is to ensure that a field researcher's perceptions are empirically grounded instead of being fashioned out of inadequate or faulty knowledge (Blumer, 1980, p. 412).

The strategy of exploration can involve observation, interviewing, life histories, and the study of official and personal documents (Hammersley, 1989, p. 158). More emphatically, Hammersley continues, one should "sedulously seek participants in the sphere of life who are acute observers and who are well-informed." Blumer assures us,

[s]uch a group, discussing collectively their sphere of life and probing into it as they meet one another's disagreements, will do more to lift the veils covering the sphere of life than any other device that I know of. (Hammersley, 1989, p. 158, citing Blumer, 1969, p. 41)

In today's parlance, such "focus groups" alone are sometimes sufficient to answer one's theoretical questions. Such an approach, I suggest, indicates an enormous and powerful respect for the dignity and opinions of research "subjects." With such intensive collection of data and insights, it is no wonder that Blumer insists that the method involves "a continuing interaction between guiding ideas and empirical observation" (Blumer, 1977, p. 286).

Step 3: "Inspecting" and "Dimensionalizing"

After exploration, the next stage of developing a sensitizing concept Blumer advocates is *inspection*, which brings to bear all known empirical instances to which the concept refers. In other words, does the sensitizing concept coincide with the empirical data it is intended to adumbrate? This process permits us to confirm the equivalence of the empirical instance and the sensitizing concept, a process that may lead us to revise the concept accordingly (Blumer, 1954, p. 8). It is an intensive look at all the empirical elements that make up the concept. One should imagine a broad range of empirical instances that need to be considered as key items of the concept, covering "processes, organization, relations, network of relations, states of being, elements of personal organization, and happenings" (Blumer, 1969, pp. 43-44).

When we begin to discover the variety of empirical elements that a concept adumbrates, we must attempt to outline their interrelationships, or, as Anselm L. Strauss (1987, pp. 14-16) suggests, to *dimensionalize*. Every experience or event has attributes. In a study of the social organization of hospitals (Strauss, Fagerhaugh, Suczek, & Wiener, 1985, p. 56), researchers dimensionalized *pain* in terms of its machine-causal attributes. Some machines cause pain external to the body, others internal. The connection of machines to patients ("connecting work") can be temporary or long lasting, fragile or durable, and safe or dangerous. Patients may experience the machine connection as discomforting, painful, or distasteful. The connection can be with a single machine or may involve many simultaneously. Some patients bear pain with their foreknowledge of its eventual, long-term benefits, whereas others, such as small children, have no knowledge of the imputed long-term benefit of the procedure causing the pain. These examples show how dimensionalization can be a simple but effective way to elicit substantial amounts of social data.

Once dimensionalization has fully taken place, the researcher can move on and employ the "constant comparative method" as a means to weigh the implications of the concept in various other empirical contexts or social settings. *The Discovery of Grounded Theory* (Glaser & Strauss, 1967, pp. 101-115) presents this detailed procedure as a means to develop sensitizing concepts, whereby various categories are constantly compared and contrasted as the data are being assembled. We can see the use of this method as trying to fill in as much knowledge as we can about a particular social process. John Lofland (1970, p. 38) sees the constant comparative method as a means of making interactionist concepts "more lush." Through the use of the constant comparative method, categories are so saturated with data (Strauss, 1987, p. 25) that the sensitizing concept becomes more refined and, perhaps, more applicable to other categories of data.

I see the constant comparative method as the high road to theoretical analysis. As Glaser and Strauss emphasize, the first approach to data analysis involves extensive coding of all data, a very time-consuming and systematic process of "making the data speak." Their second approach involves "inspecting" the data in such a way that one tries to find new sensitizing concepts[3] in the light of theoretical insights developed through coding (Glaser & Strauss, 1967, p. 102). In adopting the constant comparative method, the researcher generates more sensitizing concepts, but on a much broader empirical scale.

Alejandro Portes and Julia Sensenbrenner (1993) offer, in their study of immigrant groups, a dimensionalized view of "social capital," a concept originally formulated by Pierre Bourdieu in 1979. The first source of social capital involves "value introjection" derived from moral imperatives learned during socialization; the second arises from "reciprocity transactions" consisting of "chits" based on previous good deeds to others; the third, "bounded solidarity," focuses on those circumstances that lead to the emergence of group-oriented behavior; finally, the fourth, "enforceable trust," relates to formal and substantive rationality based on modern market transactions (Portes & Sensenbrenner, 1993, pp. 1322-1327). The concept of social capital permitted Portes and Sensenbrenner to explore the experience of immigrant groups.

A further tool is theoretical sampling. Unlike random sampling, which can reduce social processes to "uninterpretable sawdust" (Miles & Huberman, 1994, p. 27), theoretical sampling is good preparation for bringing qualitative data into a theoretical scheme. Miles and Huberman (1994, p. 28) identify 16 different sampling strategies for qualitative researchers. Such "conceptually driven" sampling allows the social researcher to observe classes of events and compare them with one another. It is the initial selection of those classes of events, based on an early choice of a sensitizing concept, that permits the researcher to move forward early in this stage of research. Theoretical sampling involves selecting various subdimensions, based either on one's insights or on data (Strauss, 1987, p. 16). Deborah Kestin van den Hoonaard's study (1995a) of older widows, for example, suggests that war brides constitute a significant subdimension of her group. Strauss suggests that qualitative sampling procedures, initiated by the use of adequate sensitizing concepts, can lead to "theoretical sensitivity" (Strauss, 1987, p. 16).

Step 4: Relating to Other Social Contexts

Relating data acquired in one setting to other social contexts is one of the most rewarding aspects of constructing a sensitizing concept. This step fosters an appreciation of the sensitizing concept as an effective but simple device. When we find that Diesing's view that sensitizing concepts "are not directly derived from the culture of a *single* community" (my italics), it means that his statement refers to the crucial importance of relating the concepts to other social contexts.

It should be noted that some potential concepts may have to be rejected because they remain specific descriptions for specific situations and are not transferable to other settings. A good example is the term "making my stamps," used by some people in Atlantic Canada. To qualify for unemployment insurance payments, workers must put in a minimum amount of weeks of work. For every week of work, the worker receives his stamps to prove eligibility for payouts; this expression refers to the way people in Atlantic Canada describe the required number of needed weeks to qualify for unemployment insurance payments (Turner, 1994).

Some concepts migrate from one setting to another. "Detective work," for example, is used by professionals or experts in their attempts to make an initial diagnosis of an ailment or condition. A patient may explain that he or she is experiencing a "tingly" feeling in the fingers. The medical person tries to uncover other clues to help him or her assign a formal, medicalized, professional term. All is well with this sensitizing concept. What happens, though, when the patient purposely leaves certain clues that the doctor cannot fail to "discover"?

A proposed study (Gibson, MacDonald, & van den Hoonaard, 1994) of parents with asthmatic children provides an interesting instance of detective work. Parents of chronically ill children, including children with asthma, indicate major frustration at not being heard by health care professionals, despite the fact that these parents have built up considerable knowledge and experience in this area. It has been found that parents "bait" medical staff if they want immediate attention for their children. "Baiting" occurs when parents offer telling clues that no medical staff can ignore. Stretching the truth about a child's condition is meant to provoke the medical staff to move the asthmatic child to the front of the line in an emergency room setting. It is not only an exaggeration of an asthmatic condition of a child but also the dropping of medical clues that seem more important to medical staff. This practice of baiting has become so widespread that psychiatrists and psychologists have coined a name for it, referring to it as the Munchausen Syndrome (Berkow, 1992, pp. 1543-1544).[4] Some parents "intentionally make their children gravely ill" for the purpose of securing the attention of medical staff; one can speak of this as the "Munchausen-by-Proxy Syndrome" (Schreier & Libow, 1993, pp. xi).

We can take the concept of baiting further afield. Baiting becomes the basis for a subset of observable facts when we look at what transpires between a teacher and a parent trying to deal with a "problem" child. Some readers with school-age children who have difficulty with their teachers are familiar with the experience of a teacher first speaking alone to the parent about the nature of the "problem." After the teacher has secured a parent's agreement about what the "problem" is, the child is brought in. Now the teacher and parent present to the child a united front. What has occurred is that the teacher selected the "cues" that were more likely to arouse the parent's attention and, the teacher hopes, cooperation. This is an example of a more refined form of baiting.[5]

Once descriptions become transferrable to other contexts, we have reached an important stage in the use of sensitizing concepts, namely, the generalizability of findings. As will be noted in Chapter 6, for qualitative researchers, generalizability consists of pointing to social processes with concepts that can be applied to other social settings.

Step 5: Organizing the Same Family of Terms

Erving Goffman (1961b, p. 45) speaks of the usefulness of organizing the "same family of terms" as a means of gathering together empirically related concepts. Social anthropologist Rodney Needham underscores how we can achieve a "remarkable economy" when using symbolic classifications in the study of a family of resemblances of collective action (1979, p. 60). Even someone standing outside the social sciences, such as Ludwig Wittgenstein, an original contributor to modern-day philosophy, believes there is a great benefit in applying "family resemblances" to the study of many phenomena, such as games. There are a variety of games, including language games, that have family resemblances without necessarily sharing precisely the same characteristics (Schulte, 1992, p. 113).

We can take an example from the growing body of literature on the social organization of medical establishments, in which we can observe a whole family of concepts that connect a wide variety of empirical observations that deal with a particular form of patient-doctor relationships. The reader already is aware of one concept, "detective work," that concerns the initial relationship between a medical expert (a nurse, doctor, or other professional) and a patient.[6] The medical expert tries to account for the reporting of symptoms by a patient, trying to fit it into a medical lexicon of ailments. Some patients, having acquired experience in such settings, bait the expert by purposely exposing more urgent illness clues to be "found" by the expert. "Hospital hobos" are people with "repeated fabrication of illness, usually acute, dramatic, and convincing," who wander from hospital to hospital for treatment (Berkow, 1992, p. 1534).[7] "Doctor addicts" and "active inducers" also appear in the same family of terms as "doctor shopping."[8]

The Munchausen-by-Proxy Syndrome (Schreier & Libow, 1993, p. 7) is, as indicated earlier, a related term to describe how a person can fabricate medical problems in other people, where problems range from fevers and seizures to poisoning and asphyxiation. The problem is, incidentally, so widespread that since 1977 more than 200 professional papers have been devoted to this topic (Schreier & Libow, 1993, p. 7).

Drawing on the work by Schreier and Libow (1993, p. 10), it seems to me that we can visualize all these concepts in terms of creating false histories and symptoms of illnesses, rather than in terms of actually causing illnesses. Further observation might indicate, as in the case of the Munchausen-by-Proxy Syndrome, whether the other party to the deception was innocent or was in collusion with the one reporting the fabricated or induced illness. Nevertheless, we should be aware that it is not always possible to make such categorization clear cut, for there are reports of parents who both fabricate and create sicknesses in their children. To make matters more complex, some children may actively resist their parents' fabrication or creation of illnesses.

Our initial characterization of doctor-patient relationships as "detective work" led us to a larger range of the social phenomenon which, in turn, might lead us to consider its wider ramifications. For example, at what point do medical staff call in the police? How do medical insurance companies handle the cases? What does this phenomenon tell us about our beliefs about the relationship between parents and children?

Other Helpful Hints

John and Lyn H. Lofland, in their work *Analyzing Social Settings* (1995, pp. 160-162), offer some useful tips about how to create conceptual terms by using metaphors, irony, and "creative discernment." Metaphors considerably enhance the way we convey our intended meaning to others. One is reminded of Robert Edgerton's work, *The Cloak of Competence* (1967), which speaks to the stigma in the lives of the mentally retarded. It is as if people cover themselves with a coat that gives them a new identity, a new self.

Arlie Hochschild, in *The Managed Heart* (1983) and *The Second Shift* (1989),[9] conveys highly contrasting terms to make up effective concepts to refer, respectively, to the work in industries that rely on "friendliness" for profit and to the continuing responsibility for housework held by mothers or women who have careers outside the home. With respect to the findings in *The Managed Heart,* the "production" of a smile by flight attendants is "no more than delivering a service . . . [in which] . . . the *emotional style of offering the service is part of the service.*" Emotions must be managed, which means that some emotions must be suppressed or induced to "sustain the outward countenance" (Hochschild, 1983, pp. 5, 7). In *The Second Shift*, the home "shift" for mothers leaves them without personal control over when or what they can do, and they are less likely than fathers to do "fun" things with the children (Hochschild, 1989, pp. 8-9). In this example, Hochschild imports several significant features of the regular work shift to characterize the work of mothers at home, namely loss of control about when they want to do the work and doing things that are necessary, as opposed to unnecessary or "fun."

The Loflands also suggest using irony in getting concepts across to others. Generally speaking, ironic terms point to a discrepancy between appearance and reality, or between the manifest and latent functions of the social processes being described (Lofland & Lofland, 1995, p. 161). For example, Timothy Diamond in *Making Grey Gold: Narratives of Nursing Home Care* (1992) contrasts a low-status concept, "grey," with a high-status one, "gold," to describe the social processes that govern home care for the elderly. The title of Herbert Gans's classic *The Urban Villagers* (1962) is effective in connoting the maintenance of rural ties of kinship and friendship by Italians in urban Boston. Arlie Hochschild seems always to come up with such evocative concepts in the titles of her works, such as *The Unexpected Community* (1973), which parlays into our belief that communities are something of our own choosing, something expected, rather than a "community" in a retirement home.

A third hint in the use of a tool that the Loflands give is a "rather more modest but nonetheless important and creative device" (Lofland & Lofland, 1995, p. 162). They see it as a means of discerning new conceptual variations of established ways of looking at things. Calling them "new forms" or "creative discernment," the Loflands urge us to state them in the format of a question: What new kind of . . . is this? We can fill the ". . ." with such words as "socialization" or "organizational process" and so on. This approach is not dissimilar to Blumer's "testing the concept."

This chapter outlined the five steps in crafting sensitizing concepts, namely, the need initially to derive concepts from the participant's perspective, to "explore" and use focus groups, to "inspect" and "dimensionalize," to relate the concepts to other social contexts, and to organize families of terms. Metaphors, irony, and "creative discernment" are other useful means of creating viable sensitizing concepts. The next chapter points to the usefulness of cross-cultural settings in constructing sensitizing concepts.

NOTES

1. Dr. Daniel C. Jordan was a member of the Faculty of Education, University of Massachusetts, and founder of ANISA, an approach in education that saw learning in a holistic way. Some school boards in the Appalachians and in Connecticut adopted Dr. Jordan's philosophy and practice of education. His brutal, innocent murder in the early 1980s left many of his friends and colleagues in deep shock. My wife and I named our son after this devoted and articulate scholar and warm person.

2. In contrast, an *etic* approach "employs an external method of analysis wherein all observations are categorized by a scheme of classification which is logically prior to the observations" (Clifton, 1968, p. 308).

3. Glaser and Strauss use the term "category" to refer to the sensitizing concept (see, e.g., Glaser & Strauss, 1967, p. 102).

4. I am grateful to Dr. Paul McDonnell of the Department of Psychology at the University of New Brunswick for drawing my attention to this syndrome during one of our many informal luncheon discussions.

5. This is one way of looking at it. Some teachers may not necessarily agree with this interpretation.

6. I will deal with the term "detective work" more systematically in Chapter 6.

7. The technical literature refers to this phenomenon as the Munchausen Syndrome (Schreier & Libow, 1993).

8. Some doctors may use the term "doctor shopping" in their conversations with patients to discourage patients from seeking a second opinion, welding "real" patients with an incompetent physician (Paul McDonnell, private communication, October 6, 1995).

9. Helena Lopata's book *Occupation: Housewife* (1971), one of the first of its kind, conveys a similar metaphor.

5. CROSS-CULTURAL SETTINGS

Ever since I wanted to become a social scientist, I was drawn to Clyde Kluckhohn's famous definition of culture as a "design for living" (1949/ 1985). "A way of thought" is another definition of culture, but one that highlights its intangible nature, inasmuch as Kluckhohn's definition seems to encompass a culture's tangible dimensions. Because culture is so all-pervasive, it is difficult to understand our own culture. We abide by many taken-for-granted assumptions. Studying another culture is its mirror image: We can encounter problems *because* we do not share in that "strange," taken-for-granted world.

The ethnographers I know who have undertaken research in settings of other cultures, like myself, often confess that such research has had a profound effect on their scholarship and on them as persons. The research has never left them untouched, for better or worse, or both. In our better moments, we find ourselves referring back to our research in other cultures to highlight what has worked and even to what has not worked if it sheds light on how to avoid important mistakes the next time. We wax enthusiastic and are, we hope, wiser through insights gained in the field. We also know that there are few better teachers than the dynamic force of example. I believe that my research in Iceland is no exception in that regard; therefore, I feel it to be a matter of obligation and privilege to speak about that research as an illustration of how one can develop sensitizing concepts in cross-cultural research.

I have two tasks in this chapter that may benefit anyone who might seriously consider using the sensitizing concept. On one hand, the chapter gives a practical, in-the-field demonstration of how I went about creating sensitizing concepts in one of my research stays in Iceland.[1] On the other hand, I hope to show that doing research in a different cultural setting is actually quite helpful in developing sensitizing concepts that are applicable to one's own, familiar, culture.

No researcher should overlook the benefit of doing cross-cultural field research. The newness of the experience heightens perceptions of social relations, arouses curiosity, and brings out creative moments. Cross-cultural research allows a researcher to conduct a reflexive analysis of his or her work (Reinharz, 1992, p. 125). Some researchers, such as Stanley H. Udy, Jr., are persuaded to do cross-cultural research because it permits them to seek relatively extreme variations in comparison to their own culture and thus acquire insights about social processes that would have been hitherto invisible (Udy, 1964, p. 163).

Cross-cultural research, however, also has a downside that all researchers must take into account. Contrary to earlier assertions that it would take one or two years to become familiar with a different culture, social scientists (e.g., Reinharz, 1992, pp. 330-336) now strongly recommend shorter stays in the field. Experienced researchers are well aware of the fatigue and irritation that attend to long stays in the field. Taking hold of sensitizing concepts may be one of the most constructive and effective ways of doing cross-cultural research.

Linda Turner (1994) voices the findings of other cross-cultural researchers when she claims that developing sensitizing concepts can be "both easy and difficult at the same time":

> We might quickly identify concepts which intrigue us because they *are* different and apparent. However, we may be at a loss to a greater or lesser degree when we attempt to clarify their meaning for the person who has used the sensitizing concept. (Turner, 1994, p. 4)

Humans are creatures and creators of culture: We have the ability to absorb the taken-for-granted world of our culture. We live and breathe in a taken-for-granted world. The absorption of this taken-for-granted world is so seamless that our culture appears quite "natural" to us. Our ability to naturally learn our culture brings enormous benefits. For example, we are spared the considerable amount of time that it would take to reinvent all the intangible and tangible things that make up our culture and our identity. These advantages, however, evaporate when we assign ourselves the task of understanding our own culture—a problem that ethnomethodologists have been trying to grapple with during the past few decades.

There are some broader problems that arise out of doing cross-cultural research, related to conceptual issues in general. Words used in one culture may specify an altogether different concept in another culture. For example, in a search of North American indices of sociology journals for what scholars offer on the subject of "crowding," it is possible to read, between the lines, the assumed negative consequences of crowding, with its deleterious impact on behavior, family relations, health, sexual behavior, and other matters (see the useful index developed by Judith C. Lantz, 1987, p. 368). A European index might consider the negative impact of "wide open spaces" on human interaction (as I noted in my 1991 research on Dutch immigrants' coming to North America). It is such difficulties with theoretical language, with concepts, that counteract the potential usefulness of cross-cultural research.

Cultural filters are another well-known problem in cross-cultural field research that can play havoc not only with one's fieldnotes but also with emerging concepts. Westerners see what appears to be a highly ritualized form of politeness among Iranians called *tarof*, whereby a host thrice or more offers something to the guest, to be refused as many times. From an Iranian perspective, *tarof* has much to do with an understated way of expressing opinions, borne out of many centuries of Arab domination, whereby opinions must be couched in ways understandable to only the group. A researcher may be inclined to develop concepts of Iranian politeness far removed from the genesis and function of *tarof* (Lewis & Stevens, 1986).

It is also difficult to find conceptual equivalences, even if they are based only on terms. Herman W. Smith, a sociologist who has lived in Japan, reminds us that the Japanese term "grandfather" (*ojiisan*) indeed signifies "grandfather" in Western culture, but *ojiisan* also is used as a sign of respect for any old man (Smith, 1991, p. 499). This particular term, as simple as it is, is bound to produce conceptual confusion if we, as researchers, are unaware of those differences.

In a short monograph of this nature, I cannot be exhaustive in pointing out the conceptual dangers and promise of doing research in cross-cultural settings. The above paragraphs alert us to the problematic nature of such research and to the fact that even very simple or seemingly self-evident terms and concepts can produce major distortions in one's conceptual laboratory.

By some dint of social fact, we are, nevertheless, placed in a position of sometimes questioning some elements of our culture: There are many minor (and major) differences within our own culture that force us to see things "differently" sometimes. On the whole, we are "stuck" in our culture, held captive until a momentous event or a dramatic shift in our lives causes us to challenge our taken-for-granted assumptions. If some sociologists and anthropologists cannot wait for such unpredictable and arbitrary changes to occur, they turn to the study of a different culture. Other sociologists and anthropologists, however, have found ways of discovering and challenging the taken-for-granted world of their own culture.

There is an odd twist in the study of other cultures. We are innocently drawn by our curiosity to study another taken-for-granted world. With varying degrees of success or failure, we try to distill the essence of another culture, believing it, at first, to be unique, not universal. Some anthropologists may have chanced upon a sensitizing concept that, they believe, they can attribute to a whole culture—such as Ruth Benedict's (1959) "Apollonian" and "Dionysian" patterns of culture—only to be shown that such sweeping concepts are of limited usefulness as social scientists strive for more subtle and complex explorations of other cultures.[2] Others, such as Simon Schama (1987), a Harvard historian, use the term "embarrassment of riches" to characterize Dutch culture in its "Golden Age." Linda Turner, in discussing her thoughts about Western youth rendering aid to dissatisfied nations, finds that the concept "embarrassment of riches" may well have some analytic use in studies dealing with groups of Western youth in the Third World (Turner, 1994, p. 6).

Another facet of cross-cultural research involves a looping back to our own culture, so that we see things differently as we begin to question our taken-for-granted assumptions and trace similarities and even universals vis-à-vis our own culture. The *couvade* (Brown, 1963, p. 51), whereby men of some South and North American tribes adopt the posturing of pregnant women—a "symbolic role in the lying-in," in which they are expected to simulate labor pains and remain in bed—does not seem so unusual anymore when we realize that our culture has its own form of *couvade*, albeit greatly minimized: On cue, the father of the conceived child begins to worry about family finances during the fifth month of pregnancy. Similarly, the father's behavior in the labor, delivery, or waiting room may appear to an outsider as a good example of *couvade*, wherein a father may appear to believe that he has the "same" intense experience and expectation as the pregnant woman.

If we can draw an analogy, cross-cultural research is much like driving over a long track of dirt roads, jarring our teeth and bones. We never will feel the same again when the road becomes smooth pavement. It is this examination of other cultures, this "jarring" of our mindset, that makes it possible for us to see things in a new light—an ideal ground for generating sensitizing concepts. This looping-back effect of cross-cultural research is reminiscent of the method of comparative analysis advocated by Barney Glaser and Anselm L. Strauss (1967, pp. 117-158).

It was this particular "jarring" effect on one's conscious worldview that I had in mind when I chose Iceland as a remote culture for my first graduate degree in sociology and anthropology at Memorial University of Newfoundland.

The Icelandic Field Setting

In 1973, I undertook my second field research trip to Iceland.[3] What drove me to consider Iceland for research purposes was my interest in how remote communities on the periphery of society relate to centralized institutions. In the popular literature, writers and political commentators already were speaking of Iceland's proclivity in developing autonomous communities—fishing communities sustained by fishing fleets and fish-freezing plants owned for the most part by people in these communities. What social processes attend to this state of affairs? The problem of geography and the extension of the 200-mile fisheries limits in 1973, involving highly publicized skirmishes with English trawlers, added significance to my research problem.

The community I had selected in the extreme northwest of Iceland relied completely on its fisheries to sustain itself (van den Hoonaard, 1992). It was a community of slightly more than 3,000 people, and the town was dramatically etched in a striking landscape of glaciers and fjords. Although the town derived the most substantial part of its fishing economy from trawler fishing, with impressive catch records and processing plants, there was also a sizable contingent of shrimpfishers. The 77 shrimpfishers previously had worked on the trawlers but were ready to be their own masters by becoming owners of small shrimp-fishing vessels. The occupational ideology of the shrimpers centered on having a sense of independence, a love for individualism, and developed fishing skills. In their relationship to the community and to the central authorities, the shrimpers cultivated their ethos in a variety of ways, often stating them as something that would, ultimately, serve the public interest.

It was the larger, economically more powerful trawler and longliner fisheries that dictated the context of the shrimpers' struggles with central authorities. The struggle was not merely one of how the shrimpers could state their case as a public interest one but how the shrimpers could draw and hold the attention of politicians and biologists in Iceland's capital city, where the more powerful fisheries wielded more influence.

Geographically, Reykjavik, the seat of government and the location of 160 government institutions, lies in the south of Iceland. Increased centralization policies, which developed after World War II, made the rest of Iceland the hinterland of the capital. This hinterland supplied the capital with migrants. Communications in Iceland are unifocal; that is, Reykjavik stands at the center of the transportation network. Today, a native of Arnesysla—a district *east* of Reykjavik—would speak of going *south* when journeying to Reykjavik. This colloquialism has found its place in formal and informal usage. In a sense, the geography matters less than the political or administrative morphology of the country.

Taken symbolically, not literally, the notion of "going south" (*að fara suður* in Icelandic) reflects the relationship between an interest group in the periphery and a central institution of government. It involves a move in a geographical sense but also, more important, denotes the quality of the relationship between various peripheral groups in the country and the core government institutions.

The notion of "going south" amply illustrates the persuasive politics of marginal and remote areas in influencing centralist decisions. It signifies a specific type of action between political and administrative institutions in Reykjavik, on one hand, and local interest groups outside the capital, on the other. It consists of a personal visit of a party of representatives hoping to affect some decision so as to benefit the group. We can sum up the characteristics of "going south" as follows:

- It takes place at the initiative of those coming from outside Reykjavik.
- A crisis situation is usually the precipitating factor.
- It is resorted to when all other methods of changing government policies have proven fruitless.

The strategy of "going south" employed by the fishermen to present their case to political influentials reflects the political role of science in Icelandic society. As a result of any such pressure on centralist politicians, the Marine Research Institute may feel bound to sacrifice some of its cherished long-term projects in favor of short-term demands. The constraints imposed by the local village on the shrimp fishery are mitigated by the shrimpers' external relations with centralist institutions. By virtue of these external relations, the community of shrimpfishermen became a socially more viable and stable fishery.

Another condition that makes "going south" a reality in Icelandic politics is the ad hoc nature of public policy. The active ingredients that go into policy making are the *events* themselves, rather than a broad set of guidelines placed in the context of many years to come. Such decisions are explained "rationally" by appropriate functionaries but can best be described as ideological insofar as they purport to defend the interests and prerogatives of the bureaucracy. The visible lack of long-range planning encourages peripheral groups to make presentations and effect a change of plans.

The shrimper comparing his experience with the biologist's expertise also fits the overall configuration of "going south." Here, the emotional reaction to being on the periphery of decisions affects the shrimper intimately; the reaction is one of distrust and of invalidating anything coming from Reykjavik, including the "scientific" work of the marine biologists.[4] Marine biologists purport to be fighting against folk knowledge, or "ethnoscience," but the shrimper devalues, equally, the importance of "desk science." This oversimplified mode of viewing the marine biologist has a strong appeal to local people. The shrimpers' antiscience attitude wins easy support, especially when vindicated by the scientists' occasional lack of success at prognosis.

Discussion

Let us see how I developed the sensitizing concept of "going south," following the procedures outlined in the previous chapter.[5]

USE OF THE PARTICIPANTS' PERSPECTIVE

The term "going south" came to my attention in a variety of ways, illustrating its importance in a community's discourse when it "does business" with the centralist institutions. Everyday conversations, meetings of fishery unions, and newspaper reports and letters to the editor keep the term "going south" constantly in front of community life. It was fortunate that I could directly translate the Icelandic expression *að fara suður* without losing its meaning. Some cross-cultural settings make it very difficult to translate a foreign word. Paul Diesing (1971, p. 209) cites Redfield's frustration in not being able to translate a certain Mayan word, which he then felt best to leave untranslated. Similarly, readers familiar with the Dutch word *gezelligheid* know its concrete referent to a place that is cozy and warm but are unable to find an English equivalent.

EXPLORATION AND THE USE OF FOCUS GROUPS

I developed other lines of inquiry that involved crisis settings, and I looked at official documents, including letters exchanged between the marine biologists and shrimpfishers. Once I had ascertained the presence of "going south," I began to look for its empirical referents in meetings and news bulletins. I attended union meetings of the shrimpers when they were negotiating new contracts with local fishery-plant owners. After having obtained the names of those involved in this practice—both fishermen and marine biologists—I was able to interview them and learn more about the social organization of the fishery. I also brought up this matter with the shrimpers' families, especially those men who were often asked to go to Reykjavik.

Unfortunately, it never occurred to me at that time that I should have organized at least one focus group. I believe, in hindsight, that I would have benefited enormously from having even a handful of shrimpers available for such a consultation. My trips to the fishbanks and my routine discussions with a crew while steaming back to port also could have constituted focus groups had my attention been up to par.

INSPECTING/DIMENSIONALIZING

In developing my original sensitizing concept, I was able to bring in related terms and social processes. I brought in the term "desk science" to refer to the role of science in the management of fragile marine resources. I have purposely used the word "desk" as an integral part of my sensitizing concept, because that is how fishermen perceived the science of the marine biologists. The practice of "going south" also led to, and sustained, a particular hierarchy among the fishermen, namely a *hierarchy of skills*, whereby the most skilled fishermen had more free time on their hands, because they could reach their quotas earlier in the week. As a result, they were more likely to be asked to go to the capital to lobby the politicians and negotiate with marine biologists.

In this context, it was easy to bring in the concept of "ethnoscience" used in other contexts to refer to local knowledge that is passed off by fishermen as more credible than "desk science." Moreover, when the fishermen advocated their knowledge as the only reliable kind of knowledge, they raised that local knowledge to the status of science by "turning empiricism on its head" to defeat the scientists. If science is empirical, the fishermen argued, then surely their knowledge is scientific, because it was firmly grounded in their empiricism of fishing out at sea.

RELATING TO OTHER SOCIAL CONTEXTS

Having applied my concept of "going south" in the analysis of ongoing relationships between fishermen, scientists, bureaucrats, and politicians, I began to use the sensitizing concept to look at the structural issues of marine science in Iceland. At the social organizational level, "going south" involves fishery sectors, science, and centralist and political institutions. It must be borne in mind that the key ideas center on periphery-core relations. When one becomes "theoretically sensitive" (Glaser & Strauss, 1967, p. 46), one discovers that the concept begins to have a wider, comparative application to one's study.

What social processes could be delineated for the diminutive crustacean section at the Marine Research Institute, and what was, in fact, the structural situation of the Marine Research Institute as a whole within the governmental bureaucracy of Iceland? How did the institute articulate its findings and suggestions for constraint vis-à-vis national and local politicians? I tried to integrate my empirical data pertaining to all the fisheries in Kaupeyri,[6] and this led me to consider the nature of "going south" in the other, large-fishery, sectors in the community, as opposed to "going south" undertaken by small-fishery sectors, including the shrimpers. Periodic crises served as a second vital dimensionalizing point: Were the crises instigated by "going south," or were they rooted in the marine resource itself?

Inspecting newly established sensitizing concepts requires one to find empirical evidence elsewhere—the comparative analysis advocated by Glaser and Strauss (1967, p. 25). In this case, my earlier study in southern Iceland (van den Hoonaard, 1972) provided ample evidence of similar social processes of the community as it dealt with the capital. The usefulness of the term "going south" is reemphasized when other Icelandic communities *south* of Reykjavik employ it as well, extending beyond the fisheries into other social and political realms of Icelandic society.

The discovery and use of sensitizing concepts go a long way toward overcoming the challenge of doing cross-cultural research. We know that cross-cultural research tends to display elemental weaknesses of social science research, such as the presence of ethnocentrism and "overly uniform theorizing" (Reinharz, 1992, p. 125). Eventually, we no longer see the taken-for-granted world of the studied group or culture: Field researchers become the victims of their own success. A notable benefit of doing cross-cultural field research comes from efforts to learn a different language, with its reorientation of one's worldview. It is a stubborn world, as Blumer says (1954, p. 8), resistant to a facile understanding, especially when it involves a foreign culture. The learning of a new language is the only most opportune way of seizing hold of the participants' meanings of their world.

This chapter has provided a closer examination of an Icelandic field research setting, where I used a particular sensitizing concept, "going south," to reveal social processes that attend to relationships between peripheral and centralized institutions and groups. Chapter 6 examines the theoretical and analytical implications of sensitizing concepts.

NOTES

1. Some parts of this chapter are excerpted from van den Hoonaard (1992, Chapter 7).
2. Clifford Geertz in *Works and Lives* (1988) is particularly vexed by the use of such concepts.
3. I spent 1970-1971 in southern Iceland conducting field research for my master's thesis. The empirical focus delved into local-state relationships of a village, with a population of about 500, with Iceland's central government (van den Hoonaard, 1972). My article (van den Hoonaard, 1996) describes the factors that shaped the nature and direction of my research at that time.
4. The fairly recent establishment in the community of a branch of the Marine Research Institute is a response to the shrimp fishermen's cry for more facts available in Kaupeyri. This has mitigated the sense of distance and has contributed considerably to the cooperative arrangements that exist today between fishermen and marine biologists.
5. My former research on Iceland had already begun to describe this pattern of interaction (van den Hoonaard, 1972), but I had not yet arrived at a sensitizing concept that could express the relationship between the periphery and centralized governmental authority.
6. A fictitious name of the researched locale in northwest Iceland.

6. THEORETICAL AND ANALYTICAL IMPLICATIONS

This chapter explores some of the ways that sensitizing concepts share theoretical space with other classical or traditional sociological concepts, notably "definition of the situation," "ideal type," "typology," and "ideology," with which they share a number of similarities. Finally, we shall explore how two cognate disciplines—anthropology and psychology—have drawn their inspiration from Blumer's sensitizing concepts. Like other efforts in recent years (see, e.g., Miles & Huberman, 1994) to consider more carefully the theoretical relevance of qualitative research, the practitioners of sensitizing concepts will find it helpful to see how these concepts stack up against sociological theory. There is a special urgency to consider the theoretical relevance of sensitizing concepts, because already back in 1970, John Lofland spoke of the failed promise of qualitative social scientists to bring their respective studies to a theoretical conclusion. He spoke of his anguish that a "conceptual impoverishment" had seized the discipline then, rendering fruitless any attempt to bring one's work to a theoretical conclusion.

As Norman K. Denzin states (1977, p. 48), when proper procedures are followed, the sensitizing concept opens the door to theoretical development. The mediating element between concrete, observable phenomena, on one hand, and the discovery of sociological patterns, on the other hand, is the sensitizing concept that guides us through the process of abstraction from empirical reality (Zerubavel, 1980, p. 32).

No discussion of the theoretical implications of sensitizing concepts is complete without a look at the essential elements that distinguish qualitative research from quantitative approaches. The reader is warned that a certain artificiality governs any discussion of the differences between these two methodological/epistemological approaches in sociology. In the rough and tumble world of doing research, these methods do appear to converge at times. Moreover, we all "talk a good line": Quantitative researchers express the opinion that qualitative findings will "flesh out" their reports, and qualitative researchers will say that they are familiar with (and thereby recognize) quantitative approaches as one of many possible methods.

Qualitative and Quantitative Approaches

The use of sensitizing concepts in sociological research highlights some of the more notable differences between qualitative and quantitative approaches to the social world. Such differences are premised on several key points, namely analytic induction, the search for meanings, the avoidance of variables, the question of similarity rather than representativity, and transferability versus generalizability. The reader may find these comparisons forced or overdrawn, and certainly many researchers will find themselves in different camps over the life of their research projects. The comparisons are therefore mere illustrations of the kinds of theoretical issues that researchers may have to consider when using sensitizing concepts.

INDUCTIVE VERSUS DEDUCTIVE APPROACHES

The most serious distinction between qualitative and quantitative research involves the use of two scientific frameworks. Qualitative researchers prefer the inductive approach, whereas quantitative researchers feel more at home with the deductive framework. The interest of qualitative researchers in the analytic induction approach probably stems from the popularity of that approach among some members of the Chicago school of sociology, such as Florian Znaniecki, A. Lindesmith, and Howard S. Becker. I should point out that my attempt to differentiate the two styles of research simply as "inductive" or "deductive" can be overdrawn. Charles Ragin (1994) and others have pointed out that although formally the two approaches are distinct from each other, in practice, researchers may use both (and I use these characterizations as a means to draw attention to their epistemological differences). Qualitative researchers "use evidence to formulate or reformulate" theoretical insights, whereas quantitative researchers work up hypotheses based on previous research or a review of the literature and collect data to assess "the correctness of the hypothesis" (Ragin, 1994, p. 15) and the usefulness of the theory. Some researchers on "both sides of the House" are more likely to use retroduction, the interplay between induction and deduction (Ragin, 1994, p. 47), although it seems that qualitative researchers are more likely to engage in retroduction.[1]

The inductive approach has an important bearing on the research status of sensitizing concepts. As Grant McCracken (1988, p. 16) claims, the "qualitative goal . . . is often to isolate and define categories during the process of research," and the qualitative researcher "expects the nature and definition of analytic categories to change in the course of a [research] project." If we use concepts as a means to sensitize ourselves to the patterns and social processes inherent in the collected data, we are more likely to see them as a means to understand the subtlety and complexity of social life. For Blumer, in any case, quantitative researchers tend to use ideas and concepts without explicit reference to the concrete world. We can thus organize our provisional findings without insisting on using either a precise or an exact category too early in the research process.

MEANINGS VERSUS RATES

The second distinction between qualitative and quantitative research that implicates the use of sensitizing concepts concerns the idea that the first approach deals foremost with the *meanings* that people impute about their social world, whereas the second research approach is motivated by the purpose of obtaining *rates*, a statistical profile involving a large number of cases. If qualitative researchers have the goal of unraveling these meanings, quantitative researchers seek rates (Reinharz, 1993, p. 6). As Blumer sees it, behavior results not from "such things as [social] environmental pressures, stimuli, motives, attitudes, and ideas but instead from how researchers interpret and handle these things in the action which he is constructing" (Blumer, 1978, p. 99).

The question of meanings and rates finds its way into the problem of the generalizability of qualitative and quantitative data. In securing our subjects' meanings, we must inevitably consider their relevance to a larger population for the purpose of making generalizations, and, as a consequence, the methodological principles are quite different from when they pertain to the study of rates. I shall more closely examine these principles in a later section.

CONCEPTS VERSUS VARIABLES

At the outset, it should be stated that the term "concept" has a connotation in qualitative research different from its meaning in quantitative research. In the latter instance, concepts are not only known as variables but also are used solely for the purpose of establishing a relationship between them. Thus, in quantitative research, researchers must try to operationalize and measure concepts in very precise ways. For quantitative researchers, concepts and variables are analogous. Qualitative researchers speak of "concepts," but quantitative researchers use "variables."

I use these nomenclatures only as a means of distinguishing and talking about the nuances of qualitative and quantitative research in general. The researchers who use variables do so with the sole aim of establishing measurement and correlation of phenomena, whereas they use concepts (in the qualitative sense) to guide research and establish social processes. Thus, qualitative researchers do tend to eschew causal explanations but highlight social processes.[2] Quantitative researchers use the term "concept" as they introduce variables into their work. In this light, we should also allude to the use of concepts in a cognate discipline, psychology, where they intervene between antecedent variables, on one hand, and behavior (consequence) variables, on the other hand.

Undismayed by the rising influence of "sociological analysis which seeks to reduce human group life to variables and their relations" (Blumer, 1956, p. 683), Blumer felt bound to demonstrate, within 2 years of his first article, the shortcomings of "variable" research in his 1956 presidential address at the annual meetings of the former American Sociological Society (now the American Sociological Association). His exposition of the flawed nature of variables to understand the human, empirical world allows one to better appreciate the nature and purpose of sensitizing concepts. First, he faulted variable analysis for its seeming chaotic selection of variables, ranging from such simple ones as sex distribution to such complex ones as depression. What is noticeable is the "conspicuous absence of rules, guides, limitations, and prohibitions" (Blumer, 1956, p. 683) to govern the choice of such variables. In this connection, one is drawn to the findings of Charles M. Bonjean, Richard J. Hill, and S. Dale McLemore (1970), who explore the measurements of 78 variables, ranging from "achievement" to "work-value orientations," to realize that over a 10-year period, 1954-1965, some 2,080 scales and indices were used in scholarly journals (p. 147).

A second criticism involves the absence of generic variables, so essential to interconnect abstract categories. Blumer avers that when sociologists claim that they *do* use generic variables, these variables are far too restricting on account of historical and cultural specificity, as well as lack of uniform indicators, and are applied with considerable variability.

Third, one might say, as does Blumer (1956, p. 685), that generic variables suffer from the "here-and-now" syndrome. Let me offer the sort of example that Blumer would give to illustrate the "here-and-now" context of "variables research." In hypothesizing that New Brunswick Acadians (who speak French) vote for Liberal political candidates because of the Liberals' support for English-French bilingualism, we have reduced the reasons for voting for Liberals to variables involving ethnicity and language. The "here-and-now" syndrome is filled with operationalizing concepts that deal with localized and time-specific occurrences, stripped bare of the complexities of history, time, social atmosphere, experience with organizations, listening to rival candidates, ethical sensitivities, and many of the other realities of life. Nor do we learn about the nature and meaning of those things that led voters to choose their candidate. One challenge for quantitative researchers, as the Loflands state, is to get themselves "into [an] exclusive concern with very small problems simply because these problems are amenable to quantification" (Lofland & Lofland, 1995, p. 138). Nevertheless, qualitative researchers should not get puffed up too much about the openness of our strategies, because we are all bound to ask limited questions and come up with partial explanations. The matter of being open to achieving fuller insights about social processes is more a question of relativity rather than absoluteness.

Graham D. Rowles and Shulamit Reinharz offer an enlightening discussion of the use of both qualitative and quantitative research strategies (1988, p. 5). They consider how a qualitative approach to the study of housing for the elderly yields a different picture from a quantitative approach. They are also quick to suggest that each approach gives a partial view, is legitimate, and can be used alone or in combination. Their distinct epistemologies and philosophies are the source of the differentiated understandings of the social phenomenon.

For Blumer, the most disconcerting aspect of variable analysis resides in its inability to convey the "core of human action" (Blumer, 1956, p. 685), which is set by the process of interpretation or definition of the situation. His criticism brings us directly back to the symbolic interactionist premise that human beings act toward others and things on the basis of meanings they assign to them. The definition of the situation is "a vast digestive process" that is transmuted into social action (Blumer, 1956, p. 686). Only a scientific approach that subscribes to self-reflection is adequate to the task of recognizing the important challenges of studying the emergence and shifts of meanings and human action (cf. Baugh, 1990, p. 3).

Not only are variables empty of the interpretive dimensions of human life, but they also mistakenly, and falsely, construct a correlation where one variable is "independent" and the other "dependent." Quantitative researchers present variables as "empirical" data, whereas in fact they offer a "very abstracted view of everyday social worlds" (Mills, 1959, p. 124). A sex category, female/male, does not contain the worlds of meaning that surround women and men living in a gendered society. Because variables do not capture the interpretive moment of group life, the correlation or relationship between the two variables is illusory. Under conditions that involve the interpretation of social meaning, we would be wrong to infer that one variable "causes" another variable. For Blumer, the interpretation is a "creative process" that "constructs meanings," which are "not predetermined or determined by the independent variable" (Blumer, 1956, p. 687). In fairness to developments after Blumer's comments about variables, we should mention the rise of multivariate research, which not only tries to embed variables in a larger context of factors but also insists on correlational analysis, rather than causal.

Blumer's answer to the problems of variable analysis involves the use of sensitizing concepts. The criteria of his interpretive scheme overcome the difficulties of variable analysis by acknowledging that human group life involves a vast, diversified process of definition and is articulated inside moving social structures. It thus stands to reason that a proper methodological perspective must follow this subjectivist-other premise of social life. As a consequence, Blumer claims that our approach must include the study of human activity as seen and experienced by the people who have developed the activity. No less important is the need to use "broad and interlacing observations," rather than "narrow and disjunctive" ones.

SIMILARITY VERSUS REPRESENTATIVITY

Before qualitative and quantitative researchers can ready themselves to make a theoretical contribution to the field, they each must consider the relative importance of their empirical findings. Qualitative researchers are engaged in establishing an empirical *similarity* of their cases, whereas quantitative researchers are acutely aware that their empirical findings must be *representative* of the population as a whole. Let us consider each of these two stances.

As early as 1928, Blumer conceived the procedure of the "case method." It involved understanding an individual case by comparing and classifying data, or extracting what is universal (Blumer, 1928, p. 351).[3] Qualitative researchers see the purpose of a case study rather differently from quantitative researchers.[4] For qualitative researchers, the aim is to "describe the similarities shared by the cases in a category . . . and then appl[y] [the similarities] to other, related categories of cases" (Ragin, 1994, p. 184). Although we have initially discovered "what is unique about each empirical instance," we are now to uncover what the sensitizing concept displays in "common across many different settings" (Denzin, 1989, p. 15).

With respect to the quantitative researchers' striving for generalizations, it is important for them to consider the degree to which a sample of the population is, indeed, a random one. If that is the case, we can speak of a random sample of empirical data "representing" the population. It is not only randomness that would make one's empirical findings representative, but also a large number of cases, which would eliminate the unique and specific aspects of these findings (Ragin, 1994, p. 35).[5]

TRANSFERABILITY VERSUS GENERALIZABILITY

Once we have ascertained that our empirical findings involve either similar cases or representative samples, we can move on to consider their theoretical contribution to the field. In the case of qualitative research, sensitizing concepts can be a keystone in the arch of our theory. For quantitative researchers, it is a question of establishing correlations among variables that can lead one to make theoretical statements of a generalizable nature. Denzin (1989, p. 15) went as far as saying that the "job of sociology is to discover the forms that universally display themselves in slightly different contexts." For Thomas J. Morrione, an ardent advocate of Blumer's perspective, theory must reflect the process of emergence, lest one move "away prematurely from the world that is experienced, as it is experienced" (Morrione, 1988, p. 3).

I already have stressed the fact that qualitative researchers are deeply interested in the study of social processes that govern everyday life. Because constructing sensitizing concepts involves the study of these social processes, I suggest that for qualitative researchers, the transferability of those social processes to other settings is what makes it important for theoretical development. John and Lyn Lofland (1995, p. 159) speak of the search for *"trans-setting* patterns" (my emphasis). Barney Glaser and Anselm L. Strauss refer to this form of theoretical analysis as taking

> full advantage of the "interchangeability" of indicators, and develop[ing], as it proceeds, a broad range of acceptable indicators for categories [i.e., sensitizing concepts] and properties. (1967, p. 49)

There are several techniques available that would allow us to embark on the making of theory. One of these techniques involves "comparative analysis," to be undertaken with "evidence collected from other comparative groups" (Glaser & Strauss, 1967, p. 23). Anthropologists have relied on this technique for more than a century but have applied it to macrolevel analysis of cultures. Now qualitative researchers use the strategy with respect to smaller categories of data. For example, we already have seen how "detective work" can implicate several other settings. In what started as a case study of the initial phase of a relationship between a professional or expert and his or her client or patient, we now have established that certain properties characterize that initial relationship: The expert must diagnose the patient or client's symptoms and bring them in closer harmony to what constitutes the official or formal designation of that person's condition.

Once we have documented the sensitizing concept of detective work, we seek other social settings with illustrative cases involving professional-client relationships. We have thus transferred our empirical finding to other settings. It should be noted, at this juncture, that even in the practice of everyday life, we often transfer knowledge acquired in one setting to a new setting. A particularly useful sensitizing concept in this regard is Kathy Charmaz's "identifying moments," which refers to "telling moments filled with new self-images" (1991, p. 207). Such moments "spark sudden realizations, reveal hidden images of self, or divulge what others think." A social researcher can very easily transfer the concept of identifying moments to other settings in which someone has a sudden awareness of the new self, whether it involves a widow whose new status suddenly hits home after checking "widow" on the vital-statistics form (van den Hoonaard,

1995b) or a new university student's realization that he or she is no longer in high school. The key for researchers is to be constantly aware of the existence of concepts that can be applied widely and then to use them as needed. When we can transfer such concepts to other settings, we have made a theoretical contribution to the field.

Robert Edgerton's concept of "the cloak of competence" is another good illustration of how one sensitizing concept developed in one social context has found innumerable uses in other settings. In his study of former patients of a mental hospital, he found that such patients developed clever and stubborn techniques in passing tests to maintain an air of "normality" in everyday life (Edgerton, 1967, p. 217). These self-esteem-maintaining mechanisms involve adopting a "cloak of competence" that can be applied to other settings, such as ones that involve apprentices and students in their march toward being recognized as "competent."

Making generalizations in quantitative research requires a different practice. The researcher must establish relationships between, or among, variables. For Kenneth Hoover and Todd Donovan (1995, p. 35), generalizations "based on tested relationships are the object of science." Identifying general patterns or relationships has been one of the important goals in social research, because such research "resembles research in the hard sciences" (Ragin, 1994, p. 34). This mode of building generalizations has spilled over even into the approach taken by some qualitative researchers, who identify frequency and other rates as some of the primary building blocks of generalizations (e.g., Denzin, 1989, p. 89). These qualitative researchers not only abstract numerical data but also use triangulation to warrant generalizations.

There are other qualitative researchers, however, who have adopted the other extreme position and have eschewed generalizations of any kind, keeping their findings "descriptive." These researchers claim that the purpose of qualitative research is not to build generalizations, because, in a sense, they do not have the empirical data that would allow them to do that (McCracken, 1988, p. 17). It is quite common to find no reference to generalizations in some of the prevailing methodological texts on qualitative research (e.g., Lofland & Lofland, 1995).

Sociological Theory

When Glaser and Strauss, in *The Discovery of Grounded Theory* (1967), spoke of the important theoretical orientation of their work in terms of the discovery of theory *from data*, it seemed to them at that time that only

Robert K. Merton had alluded to this theoretical process, when he had spoken of "serendipity" in coming across "unanticipated, anomalous, and strategic" findings that give rise to a new theoretical perspective (Glaser & Strauss, 1967, p. 2). I wish, however, to refer to several other concepts in sociology that appear to be similar to the sensitizing concept and accomplish the same theoretical purpose.

In accounting for the fact that ethnographers sometimes are viewed as "conscientious journalists or literate laymen" (Lofland, 1970, p. 37), producing detailed, descriptive case studies, Erving Goffman once expressed the explicit untheoretical nature of ethnographic work when he opined in *Asylums* (1961a, p. xiv) that it is "[b]etter, perhaps, [to have] different coats to clothe the children well than a single splendid tent in which they all shiver." Thus, before the post-Blumerian epoch (see Fine, 1990), it was common to find ethnographers expressing reluctance to reap theoretical insights from their work. They saw themselves as "engaged in description rather than abstract theorizing," no doubt as a result of an overreaction to positivism (Hammersley, 1985, p. 254). Lofland also complained about the ethnographer's tendencies not to follow through with analysis and coined the term "analytic interruptus" (Lofland, 1970). In recent years, an important shift has begun in ethnographic research—a move from what appears to be an atheoretical approach to a more explicit theoretical stance.

The question remains: How can the use of sensitizing concepts contribute to the development of theory and produce analytical perspectives (cf. Hammersley, 1989, p. 177)? It should be evident to the reader that the creation of sensitizing concepts involves taking distance from the data. Eviatar Zerubavel, in his attempts to link Simmel's theory of social form to field research,[6] recognizes the value of using sensitizing concepts to induce theoretical insights. If indeed, as Zerubavel (and Simmel) claim, the purpose of sociological theory is to "transcend the concreteness of reality," a process of abstracting from that reality must occur (Zerubavel, 1980, p. 27). Sensitizing concepts, following Zerubavel, are "indispensable" as the major tool to "factor out sociological patterns from the actuality of their concrete contexts" (1980, p. 31). Sensitizing concepts are thus "analytically derived, but set apart from the particulars of the setting" (Fine, 1990, p. 140). For Paul Diesing (1971), sensitizing concepts are the bridge between the worlds of observation and theory, as are all concepts. Sensitizing concepts such as "ritual," "role," and "community" have become the "basic component of holistic theories" (Diesing, 1971, p. 209).[7]

The first step in theorizing requires one to take some distance from the data. Under such circumstances, the adoption of sensitizing supra-concepts that straddle or aggregate a larger number and type of data becomes very useful. For example, "role conflict" represents such a supra-sensitizing concept. At this stage, one could start pulling in empirical findings from other research. For someone like Erving Goffman (1967, p. 194), an entire family of terms can migrate to other research settings.

Grounded theory offers the equivalent of sensitizing supra-concepts when it talks about "focused coding." The data are sorted according to an analytical scheme, primarily by developing categories of data and by showing relationships among these categories (Charmaz, 1973, p. 118). The adoption of sensitizing supra-concepts will facilitate the process that links micro phenomena to macro structural dimensions. This orientation may go a long way in answering those questions about sensitizing concepts that trouble such noteworthy critics as Jonathan Turner (1978, p. 402). Let us turn to some of the more conventional concepts in sociology that will deepen our understanding of the sensitizing concept, namely "definition of the situation," "ideal type," *Verstehen,* "typology," and "ideology." These concepts have been employed very usefully in the social sciences, and we can take advantage of them by comparing and contrasting them with sensitizing concepts.

The "definition of the situation" is very clearly a participant's understanding of his or her setting; it provides the participant's concept of the world within a particular context. As Goffman avers, when "an individual appears before others, he knowingly and unwittingly projects a definition of the situation, of which a conception of himself is an important part" (1959, p. 242). An individual's definition of the situation is but one element of expectations and behaviors in a series of nonlinear ones, whereby a researcher "must grasp the actor's definition of the situation, how he locates himself within the context, what he wants to do, the expectations he projects to others, and the choices he makes from the alternatives he notices" (Shibutani, 1988, p. 24). In a sociological sense, the definition of the situation provides a presensitizing concept. A sensitizing concept encapsulates an individual's definition of the situation, bringing it alive in consonance with other aspects of the individual's perceptions and behavior.

Some scholars, such as Randall Collins, remind us that Blumer's sociology (and his use of sensitizing concepts) looks like an elaboration of the "definition of the situation" of W. I. Thomas (Collins, 1994, pp. 261-262). Nevertheless, we should be careful when we try to size up "definition of the situation," examining such issues as whose situation is assessed, how precise its meaning is, and whether it is sufficiently clear (Becker, 1988, p. 15).

The "ideal type" also offers a comparative glimpse of the value of using sensitizing concepts. The value of dimensionalizing lies in the fact that we may acquire a clearer understanding of the various empirical components of the sensitizing concept. In our attempts to dimensionalize, the sensitizing concept functions like Max Weber's ideal type (Weber, 1949, pp. 90-93). Several scholars, particularly Barry Hindess (1972, p. 3), have pointed out that the use of ideal types copes with the problem of the subjective meanings of action.[8] Ideal types are methodological devices for "determining individual historical significance or 'meaningfulness' as a part of a procedure of reliving, introspection, or *Verstehen*" (Martindale, 1959, p. 59).

As a synthesis of many diffuse and discrete individual phenomena, the ideal type is, above all, a mental construct. In this imagined world, one has selected observational elements to construct an empirically possible world (Martindale, 1959, p. 70). The key notion of ideal types as configurations of meaningfulness is critical, for ideal types guide the "emphatic reliving of cultural and historical experience" (Martindale, 1959, p. 81).

The way in which sensitizing concepts match ideal types involves labeling or designating the diversified process of definition and meaning. They both attempt to capture definitions and meanings. They both are mental constructs derived from the participants' and the social scientists' understanding of a given social phenomenon. In some respects, ideal types are roughly equivalent to "dimensionalizing," which involves making further distinctions about categories of observations, "either by thinking about previous observations or making new ones" (Strauss, 1987, p. 14). The major point of departure between ideal types and sensitizing concepts is that sensitizing concepts are more likely to take into account the research participants' perspective; ideal types seem to be more concrete or inflexible descriptions by researchers of the social phenomenon.

Another important methodological (and theoretical) contribution is the notion of *Verstehen,* a term used by Max Weber to develop sociological categories. In Weber's own words, *Verstehen* involves understanding

> in terms of *motive* the meaning an actor attaches to [a] proposition [such as a mathematical] proposition . . ., when he states it or writes it down, in that we understand what makes him do this at precisely this moment and in these circumstances. (Weber, 1949, p. 95)

For Weber, *Verstehen* is a "rational understanding of motivation" (Weber, 1949, p. 95). The avenue to achieve this understanding, according to

Emmet and MacIntyre (1970, p. 9), is largely the result of a process of acculturation, much like the "commonsense experience of the so-called natural world."

Verstehen does not indicate individual motivation, shared meanings as to what constitutes the motivation of individuals, what social scientists understand what those meanings are, or a reconstruction of the individual meaning systems of those whom they study (Truzzi, 1974, p. 4). *Verstehen* is not simply about the insights that researchers gain about the research participant's behavior; it is about the cognitive insights that the participant has about his or her action (cf. Truzzi, 1974, p. 102). Since the mid-1960s, sociologists (and many anthropologists) have been working to incorporate *Verstehen* into their qualitative approaches. As Gary Alan Fine underscores, Weber's notion of *Verstehen* has an enormous appeal for interactionists, because it attempts to understand the world from the inside (Fine, 1990, p. 141).

If *Verstehen* concerns understanding the "subjective meaning of action" (Weber, 1964, p. 96), then sociologists must concern themselves with both conscious and unconscious motives.[9] In this context, a person's explanation of what his motives might have been becomes the focus of our research—the construction of one's "motives," which is similar to the vocabulary of motives of which Kathleen Kalab (1987) speaks. Taking a further distance from motives, Arlie Hochschild (1989, p. 14), in her work on the dilemmas of the wage-earning mother, speaks of "shallow" ideologies that are contradicted by deeper feelings, as opposed to "deep" ideologies that are strengthened by deeper ones. In that same study, she uses the term "strategies of incompetence" to describe and express the motivation of women to induct traditional men into doing more housework. One such strategy was being "sick" (Hochschild, 1989, p. 51). This strategy, incidentally, undergirds the motivation of such colleagues as myself to distance themselves from the administrative work of their departments.

"Typology" is another concept in the social sciences that deserves our attention as a means of grasping the nature and aim of using sensitizing concepts. Qualitative researchers, whether they rely on interview data or other methods of the field, often are seen doodling on napkins in coffee shops. What they may be doing is making sketches of their data, trying to systematize interrelationships, and attempting to find concepts that are meaningful and data specific. It is my guess that they are working on a typology to make their analysis

more systematically coherent, and, by showing the logical possibilities . . . [and] . . . sometimes call[ing] attention to existing but unnoticed patterns or to the empirical absence of a logically possible pattern. (Lofland & Lofland, 1995, p. 126)

In our attempts to develop a typology, we try to ascertain the variations, whether subtle or explicit, in the data we have collected (see, e.g., Hammersley & Atkinson, 1983, p. 181). When the data are sufficiently rich, our eyes and minds begin to focus on categories of these data and to place them on a continuum. When that happens, a researcher will be inclined to set out these categories in a visual manner. Resisting the temptation to develop a typology too early in the data collection phase, the researcher can map out those categories for which there are insufficient data. A premature attempt to develop a typology may unnecessarily force the researcher to make the data fit the typology, thereby overlooking the emergence of other kinds of categorical data.

The visual layout that a typology requires forces our gaze toward the spaces that are vacant of data.[10] Although we must try to find and posit data in every space, we should be aware that a typology (with its logical dividing up of space) cannot always be filled with data. Our attempts at being logical can easily outrun the data. As Lofland warns us, the building of a typology "can easily become a sterile exercise":

> Unless performed within the context of full and extensive knowledge of and sensitivity to the actual setting, it will reveal little or nothing. Arbitrary box building is not a substitute for a close feel for the actual circumstances. (Lofland & Lofland, 1995, p. 126)

Sociological research is filled with the successful application of typologies to data, often starting with a sensitizing concept. Many readers are familiar with "awareness contexts" to signify relationships among medical personnel, hospital patients, and others, brought on by the sometimes uneven distribution of information about a dying patient (Glaser & Strauss, 1964). Robert Merton's (1938) "modes of individual adaptation" involving an individual's acceptance, rejection, or substitution of societal goals or institutional means is another well-known typology. In Chapter 3, we became acquainted with a typology derived from the Hawthorne Electric Plant studies, in which the men in the Bank-Wiring Room held opinions about behavior, ranging from desirable or undesirable. "Ratebusters" were too eager, "chisellers" performed too little work, and "squealers" were those who reported to a supervisor (Roethlisberger & Dickson, 1961, p. 522). As can be inferred, typologies are not ends in themselves but are very simple, but highly effective ways, of ensuring that a sensitizing concept does indeed contain all the dimensions of empirical referents.

Finally, "ideology" as a conceptual tool deserves attention as a means for understanding the use of sensitizing concepts. There are a variety of ways that we define ideology. Karl Mannheim offers a widely applicable definition, namely, the "varying ways in which objects present themselves to the subject according to the differences in social settings" (1936/1972, p. 238). These "mental structures" are the object of sociological investigation and invite attention to examining the concrete ways in which society embeds them in daily life.

When we pay attention to the folk terms used by research participants, we gain a sense of the ideological underpinnings of their lives and history. The sort of research we engage in when we use sensitizing concepts is driven by our efforts to understand the worldview, perspective, or "ideology" of the people we study. If we regard folk terms as expressing an ideological point of view, we are left raising the following relevant questions and issues. If folk terms indeed sustain a particular "false" conscious or semiconscious view of the world (Mannheim, 1936/1972, p. 238), how do we present ourselves in ways that do not delude ourselves? What is the task of the folk term with respect to the larger society? Careful attention must be paid by the social investigator to the language employed in the folk term and brought to account within the framework of the larger social milieu.

The folk term "military brats" serves to lessen the overall stature of the military and military families in particular. The military, along with the police, is the state's machinery that is legitimately entitled to use force or violence. This involves tremendous responsibilities and shapes the way the state assigns expenditures and exclusive prestige to the military. Military families derive their social position from this fact, and this has a pronounced influence on public opinion. The term "military brat" may well serve in this case to undermine the prestigious position of the military, making military families more amenable to a closer integration with civil society.

After considering the various above-mentioned concepts, we should turn to some of sociology's cognate disciplines, especially anthropology and psychology, to find echoes of the use of sensitizing concepts.

Cognate Disciplines

It is important to remember that Blumer's "distinctive humanistic perspective will likely remain as one of his most enduring contributions, not just to sociology, but to all disciplines searching for a better understanding of human association and group life" (Morrione, 1988, p. 11). The sensitizing concept constitutes a concrete reminder that human action is forged and maintained through ordinary, everyday, human interaction.

The absorption of the sensitizing concept by other disciplines is a remarkable tribute to Blumer, who proposed in 1940 that the term "adjustment" (to describe the ever-emergent social process) be used as a "pivotal" concept in social psychology, social anthropology, and cultural sociology (Morrione, 1988, p. 10).

ANTHROPOLOGY

Sociological ties to anthropology remain important. As Van Maanen (1988, p. 14) claims, the "aims, means, and problems" of both fields are similar. It stands to reason that ethnographic conceptions in one field would easily spill over to the other. It should be noted, however, that the status of ethnography differs radically in each field (Van Maanen, 1988, p. 21): For anthropologists, it is *the* field; for sociologists, ethnography occupies a marginal, although sometimes a mythlike, status.

Anthropology has its roots in methodological positivism, where cultures are human collectivities, to be arranged, sorted, studied, and cataloged, much like a species of butterflies. Now, however, positivism has become the "epithet of choice" (Plath, 1990, p. 383). The interpretive framework in anthropology was developed in the 1970s, both in reaction to the positivist stance and as a recognition of the role of interpretation of culture. Stanford M. Lyman and Arthur J. Vidich (1988) provide us with an overview of Blumer's career, and both Elvi Whittaker (1994) and R. F. Ellen (1984, pp. 26-30) examine Blumer's contribution to anthropology. Anthony Cohen's work *The Symbolic Construction of Community* (1985) represents a more recent example of this approach. When Clifford Geertz (1988, p. 1) baldly states that the "illusion that ethnography is a matter of sorting strange and irregular facts into familiar and orderly categories . . . has long since been exploded," researchers might well dwell on sensitizing concepts as a tool.

We already have indicated, in Chapter 3, the anthropological term "experience-near" to describe those things that can lead to the use of the sensitizing concept. Derived from Heinz Kohut's work in psychoanalysis (Geertz, 1983, p. 57), the term fits easily into our discussion of sensitizing concepts. As desirable as the term is, Geertz is nervous about the use of experience-near concepts: "Confinement to experience-near concepts leaves an ethnographer awash in immediacies, as well as entangled in vernacular" (1983, p. 57). Similarly, the use of "experience-distant" concepts "leaves him [the anthropologist] stranded in abstractions and smothered in [anthropological] jargon" (Geertz, 1983, p. 57). For Geertz, one must grasp experience-near concepts and place them in "illuminating" connection with experience-distant concepts (Geertz, 1983, p. 58). This "delicate" approach, one hopes, will capture the general features of social life.

I have found R. F. Ellen's treatment of the "interpretive paradigm" disappointing, because despite the recognition of the importance of this paradigm, Ellen still emphasizes a priori conceptual analysis. Anthropologist Gerald Berreman (1962) was particularly effective in promoting such concepts as "impression management" in anthropological field research, and applying them to the Indians' response to him as an ethnographer. Berreman avers that, in his case, the concept of impression management was a good research tool, because he was working in a highly stratified society that begot impression management strategies. According to Jonathan Turner (1978), sensitizing concepts reverberate the symbolic interactionist's lack of attention to social structural dimensions, but Turner has otherwise seen much benefit in the use of the symbolic interactionist paradigm, including sensitizing concepts, in the study of social organization (1978, p. 401). His deliberate attempts to make symbolic interactionism work in anthropological field settings makes his criticism of sensitizing concepts a critical one: If sensitizing concepts cannot "account for more complex forms of social organization, pursuit of its strategy will preclude theorizing about much of the social world" (Turner, 1978, p. 402).

The main thrust of the new subjectivist approach to the study of culture started when *emic* approaches, namely, the goal of acquiring an understanding of the studied culture from the perspective of its members or insiders, became accepted (as opposed to *etic* approaches). This procedure developed after the 1950s (Ellen, 1984, p. 79) when anthropologists laid the groundwork for ethnoscience. The purpose is to create cultural grammars that would provide the necessary tools to participate in the studied culture (Ellen, 1984, p. 79), much like a non-French speaker would have to acquire some knowledge of French grammar before starting to speak the language. Such an approach would require us to develop "indigenous categories and concepts" (Ellen, 1984, p. 79).

PSYCHOLOGY

As Tamotsu Shibutani (1988, p. 30) and many others have indicated, psychologists (and economists for that matter) are less inclined to use sensitizing concepts and adopt the humanistic approach for which they stand. Since 1950, psychology has experienced a relentless wave of positivism and experimentation—hardly fertile ground for advocating the use of sensitizing concepts. There is, nevertheless, hope. No approach to the study of human beings is impermeable to change. There are scientists (by whatever name) in any discipline who, through force of circumstances or happenstance, find themselves faced with an extraordinary range of human behavior and social "fabrication" (sociologists call this "social construction"). Because it is difficult to operationalize the relevant concept, let alone to "explain" it, psychologists are beginning to recognize the dialectical, constructionist aspects of behavior. We already have referred to the Munchausen-by-Proxy Syndrome (Schreier & Libow, 1983), brought in to demonstrate a number of related sensitizing concepts.[11] Taking a wider scope, ecological psychology is gradually becoming accepted as yet another way of examining the world through psychological eyes (see, e.g., Bronfenbrenner, 1989). This approach considers the wider system of social relations and institutions that impinges on, or fosters, psychological states. The approach also seems less insistent in its emphasis on the study of variables. Paradigms have a way of experiencing sudden shifts. It will be a matter of deep interest to see whether positivism will lose its hold on psychology.

This chapter has, I hope, demonstrated that sensitizing concepts are not only central to the qualitative approach to research but also potentially critical in the shaping of theory in general. With respect to their use in qualitative methods, sensitizing concepts fit well into the inductive framework, designed to capture the meanings that humans assign to what they think, perceive, and do. As a conceptual tool, sensitizing concepts serve the function of abstracting empirical findings. It is also noteworthy that these concepts are derived from similar empirical referents, with the theoretical focus of transferring the findings about social processes to other social settings. These are modest theoretical goals, to be sure, but they have proven to be a source of many insights that have guided social researchers since the mid-1950s.

The theoretical origins of the sensitizing concept, however, can be traced back to Georg Simmel, the works of W. I. Thomas ("definition of the situation"), and Max Weber ("ideal type" and *Verstehen*). We may even venture to say that the close affinity of sensitizing concepts with the use of typologies stretches the origins of these concepts to Ferdinand Tönnies and Emile Durkheim. With such a lineage, the users of sensitizing concepts can remain confident that this method will continue to remain a backbone of both insightful and relevant research for a long time to come.

It is time to review this book's exploration of sensitizing concepts. Sensitizing concepts have proved to be an enduring part of the sociological landscape. Sensitizing concepts announce the aridity, epistemological difficulty, and consequences of "variable research." The sensitizing concept has found a life in various branches of the sociological enterprise, such as in grounded theory, the mountains of concepts discussed by Erving Goffman, the special use of the focus group, and the "new ethnographies." Methodological textbooks and studies persistently use the sensitizing concept without identifying it as such. The popularity of qualitative approaches is the driving force behind this rediscovery of sensitizing concepts. The reemergence of qualitative research, either through its discovery by seasoned researchers or through the interest of novice sociologists, obligates us to consider the strengths and weaknesses of sensitizing concepts.

The sensitizing concept not only is a pervasive technique in sociological literature, but its use also may guide us through modern life. Donald N. Levine speaks of modern-day forms that characterize contemporary life—a view he takes from Georg Simmel, the conceptual anvil of the Chicago school of sociology, the home of the sensitizing concept. In modern life, Levine notes, social forms hardly have the time to establish themselves (Levine, 1971, p. xl). The succession of old forms to new forms is so rapid that, in effect, "formlessness will be the dominant theme of life" (Levine, 1971, p. xl). Even durable forms of social organization, such as bureaucracies, corporations, laws, schools, and organized religion, and other institutions of modern society are increasingly exhibiting sudden shifts and swings. With formlessness comes more fluid and tentative ideas about what constitute "facts" and social reality. This modern social reality calls for an orientation that takes such fluidity and tentativeness into account. Sensitizing concepts seem ideal for this task. Because it is no longer possible to take into account objectivized forms of culture, we must turn to working with sensitizing concepts; through them, we can take the formlessness, fluidity, and tentativeness in stride.

Throughout its 40-year life, many have claimed that the sensitizing concept suffers from irreparable weaknesses. How does the sensitizing concept account for social structure? Is the sensitizing concept a vague notion? Is the sensitizing concept more nominal than real? Does the sensitizing concept restrict our range of data collection, and does it run the risk of going stale? Whatever merit criticisms might have, the sensitizing concept fits neatly in the hands of those researchers who wish to maintain an open attitude toward data and relish the opportunity of developing theory from the ground up.

One metaphor of the sensitizing concept sees the heart of the benefits derived from the use of sensitizing concepts as related to their ability to become halfway houses between the empirical world and theoretical abstraction. Concepts closest to the research participant's perspective are denoted as folk terms, mini-concepts, first-order concepts, experience-near concepts, situated vocabularies, or concrete concepts—they all express the natural attitude of research participants.

Sensitizing concepts have five-fold referents, involving (a) the subjects' construction of meaning about their *own* experience, (b) the subjects' construction about experience in relation to others, (c) the others' construction of the subjects' experience, (d) the researcher's construction of meaning that implicates only the subject, or (e) the researcher's construction of meaning that implicates both the subject and the other.

The use of sensitizing concepts as halfway houses should not close our eyes to the fact that sensitizing concepts migrate. We can go as far as saying that even though some concepts are conceived by the research participants, they acquire a more general character. Frequently, folk concepts become sensitizing concepts of a higher order. More to the point, we can generalize some sensitizing concepts to other social settings. For this reason, sensitizing concepts are so highly transferable that they constitute a parallel model of explaining social behavior in other social settings.

Despite the fact that there are few guidelines available about how to go about constructing a sensitizing concept, it is clear that a number of steps should be followed to ensure the development of a sound concept. The direction of these steps is toward reconciling particular empirical referents with universal social forms. The concept must be derived from the participants' perspective, explored in focus groups, "inspected" and "dimensionalized," and, finally, related to other contexts. The researcher can, moreover, make effective use of some of the informal techniques offered by John and Lyn Lofland, in particular. These involve the use of contrasting terms and irony, among other methods.

Cross-cultural settings provide a hospitable environment to develop sensitizing concepts, because it is easier to develop such concepts in a world that we are not able to take for granted. In field settings, the researcher can be creative as he or she maximizes the learning of a new language to further his or her understanding of the social setting. Equally important, the development of a sensitizing concept in another culture may well loop back to one's own culture and give rise to a greater awareness of social processes taking place there.

I have tried to demonstrate this approach with my discussion of my field research in Iceland, where the concept of "going south" encapsulates what goes on in the relationship between peripheral groups and centralist institutions. "Going south" as a sensitizing concept has several virtues, the most important one being that it speaks to the social structural dimensions of the way Icelandic society handles fundamental issues in public policy. The fact that macrolevel issues can be addressed by sensitizing concepts should make it possible to develop a clear body of concepts suited to the study of larger society.

No theoretical consideration of sensitizing concepts is complete without reference to discussing the notable differences between qualitative and quantitative approaches. Qualitative methodology is primarily inductive, dwells on meanings, uses (sensitizing) concepts, stresses similarity of empirical findings, and sees the importance of being able to transfer the findings and concepts to other settings. This approach is at the heart of qualitative theorizing. In contrast, quantitative approaches speak to deductive data gathering, involve rates and variables, must ensure representativity of the data, and proceed to making generalizations as a form of theorizing.

In this context, there are considerable affinities of sensitizing concepts within the field of sociology, namely analytic deduction, definition of the situation, ideal types, typology, and ideology. We also have considered other fields that are susceptible to the use of sensitizing concepts, notably anthropology and psychology.

The use of sensitizing concepts will allow some of us to rediscover the sociological imagination that excited us as we discovered the many social worlds that make up our society. For our purposes, the use of sensitizing concepts can be a fulfilling practice that can make us less likely to escape our readers' judgment about our work (Reinharz, 1992) and orient us to the "central and continuing task of understanding the structure and the drift, the shaping and the meanings [and] the terrible and magnificent world of human society" (Mills, 1959, p. 225).

NOTES

1. In my experience, qualitative researchers (as a minority among social science researchers) are more likely to be familiar with quantitative approaches than the other way around. I am grateful to Deborah K. van den Hoonaard for pointing this out to me.

2. In the light of this analytical streak, some would say that qualitative researchers are "poets of the human condition" (Noel Iverson, private communication, October 9, 1995).

3. I am indebted to Martyn Hammersley (1989, p. 140) for finding this relevant passage in Blumer's doctoral thesis.

4. For some quantitative researchers, a case study is, of necessity, "descriptive" and "exploratory," or represents an "initial test" of a hypothesis (see, e.g., Dixon, Bouma, & Atkinson, 1987, pp. 107-108).

5. There are, however, limitations that reside in any generalizing claim, namely the role of nonvolunteers in a study and measurement problems (Pyke & Agnew, 1991, p. 111).

6. I have derived the subtitle of this monograph, "Analytical Field Research," from the article by Zerubavel (1980). This work by Zerubavel is but one of several in the strain of "new ethnographies" that have fostered a more theoretical orientation. I am grateful to Gary Alan Fine (1990, p. 140) for pointing me in Zerubavel's direction.

7. Some of Diesing's examples (1971, p. 209) of sensitizing concepts do not conform to the criteria I have set out in this monograph, namely that they must be derived from the participants' perspective and must point to a social process (see Chapter 4).

8. See also Schutz (1972, p. xvii).

9. Weber (1964, p. 97) gives a lucid explanation of a person's construction of motives.

10. Richard Hessler (1992, p. 59) makes reference to a typological tool, "property space," developed by Allen Barton.

11. Howard Brody (1987) deepens our understanding of the "sick role" in literary prose. We can read works such as Brody's with profit as we try to shape our conceptual insights about "detective work," "baiting," and other concepts.

REFERENCES

Agar, M. H. (1980). *The professional stranger: An informal introduction to ethnography.* New York: Academic Press.

Albas, D., & Albas, C. (1994). Studying students studying: Perspectives, identities, and activities. In M. L. Dietz, R. Prus, & W. Shaffir (Eds.), *Doing everyday life: Ethnography as human lived experience* (pp. 273-289). Misssisauga, Ontario, Canada: Copp Clark Longman.

Arensberg, C. M., & Kimball, S. T. (1965). *Culture and community.* New York: Harcourt, Brace, & World.

Atkinson, P. (1984). Training for certainty. *Social Science and Medicine, 19,* 949-956.

Baugh, K., Jr. (1990). *The methodology of Herbert Blumer: Critical interpretation and repair.* Cambridge, UK: Cambridge University Press.

Becker, H. S. (1958). Problems of inference and proof in participant observation. *American Sociological Review, 23,* 652-660.

Becker, H. S. (1970). *Sociological work: Method and substance.* Chicago: Aldine.

Becker, H. S. (1988). Herbert Blumer's conceptual impact. *Symbolic Interaction, 11,* 13-21.

Benedict, R. (1959). *Patterns of culture* (9th ed.). Boston: Houghton Mifflin.

Berg, B. L. (1995). *Qualitative research methods for the social sciences* (2nd ed.). Boston: Allyn & Bacon.

Berkow, R. (Ed.). (1992). *The Merck manual of diagnosis and therapy.* Rahway, NJ: Merck Research Laboratories.

Berreman, G. D. (1962). *Behind many masks: Ethnography and impression management in a Himalayan village* (Monograph No. 4). Ithaca, NY: Society for Applied Anthropology.

Bierstedt, R. (1959). Nominal and real definitions in sociological theory. In L. Gross (Ed.), *Symposium on sociological theory* (pp. 121-144). New York: Row, Peterson, and Co.

Blumer, H. (1928). *Method in social psychology.* Unpublished doctoral dissertation, University of Chicago.

Blumer, H. (1931). Science without concepts. *American Journal of Sociology, 36,* 515-533.

Blumer, H. (1940). The problem of the concept in social psychology. *American Journal of Sociology, 45,* 707-719.

Blumer, H. (1954). What is wrong with social theory? *American Sociological Review, 19,* 3-10.

Blumer, H. (1956). Sociological analysis and the "variable." *American Sociological Review, 2,* 83-90.

Blumer, H. (1966). Sociological implications of the thought of George Herbert Mead. *American Journal of Sociology, 71,* 535-544.

Blumer, H. (1969). *Symbolic interactionism: Perspective and method.* Englewood Cliffs, NJ: Prentice Hall.

Blumer, H. (1973). A note on symbolic interactionism. *American Sociological Review, 38,* 797-798.

Blumer, H. (1977). Comments on Lewis' "The classic American pragmatists as forerunners to symbolic interactionism." *Sociological Quarterly, 18,* 285-289.

78

Blumer, H. (1978). Society as symbolic interaction. In J. G. Manis & B. N. Meltzer (Eds.), *Symbolic interaction: A reader in social psychology* (3rd ed., pp. 97-103). Boston: Allyn & Bacon.

Blumer, H. (1980). Mead and Blumer: The convergent methodological perspectives of social behaviorism and symbolic interactionism. *American Sociological Review, 45,* 409-419.

Bogdan, R. (1988). *Freak show: Presenting human oddities for amusement and profit.* Chicago: University of Chicago Press.

Bolton, C. D. (1981). [Review of *The view from Goffman,* edited by Jason Ditton]. *Contemporary Sociology, 10,* 696-697.

Bonjean, C. M., Hill, R. J., & McLemore, S. D. (1970). Continuities in sociological measurement. In N. K. Denzin (Ed.), *Sociological methods: A sourcebook* (pp. 144-150). New York: McGraw-Hill.

Brody, H. (1987). *Stories of sickness.* New Haven, CT: Yale University Press.

Bronfenbrenner, U. (1989). Ecological systems theory. In R. Vasta (Ed.), *Annals of child development* (Vol. 6, pp. 187-249). Greenwich, CT: JAI.

Brown, I. C. (1963). *Understanding other cultures.* Englewood Cliffs, NJ: Prentice Hall.

Charmaz, K. (1973). *Time and identity: The shaping of selves of the chronically ill.* Unpublished doctoral dissertation, University of California, San Francisco.

Charmaz, K. (1990, May). *Trust and betrayal: Lessons from chronic illness.* Paper presented at the Qualitative Research Conference, York University, Toronto, Ontario, Canada.

Charmaz, K. (1991). *Good days, bad days: The self in chronic illness and time.* New Brunswick, NJ: Rutgers University Press.

Clifton, J. A. (1968). *Introduction to cultural anthropology.* New York: Houghton Mifflin.

Cohen, A. (1985). *The symbolic construction of community.* Chichester, England: Ellis Horwood.

Collins, R. (1994). *Four sociological traditions.* New York: Oxford University Press.

Denzin, N. K. (Ed.). (1977). *Sociological methods: A sourcebook.* New York: McGraw-Hill.

Denzin, N. K. (1989). *The research act* (3rd ed.). Englewood Cliffs, NJ: Prentice Hall.

Denzin, N. K. (1992). *Symbolic interactionism and cultural studies: The politics of interpretation.* Oxford, UK: Basil Blackwell.

Diamond, T. (1992). *Making grey gold: Narratives of nursing home care.* Chicago: University of Chicago Press.

Diesing, P. (1971). *Patterns of discovery in the social sciences.* Chicago: Aldine Atherton.

Dietz, M. L. (1994). On your toes: Dancing your way into the ballet world. In M. L. Dietz, R. Prus, & W. Shaffir (Eds.), *Doing everyday life: Ethnography as human lived experience* (pp. 66-84). Misssisauga, Ontario, Canada: Copp Clark Longman.

Dietz, M. L., Prus, R., & Shaffir, W. (Eds.). (1994). *Doing everyday life: Ethnography as human lived experience.* Misssisauga, Ontario, Canada: Copp Clark Longman.

Dixon, B. R., Bouma, G. D., & Atkinson, G. B. J. (1987). *A handbook of social science research.* New York: Oxford University Press.

Dubin, R. (1992). *Central life interests.* New Brunswick, NJ: Transaction.

Dunham, H. W. (1970). Sociology: Natural science or intellectual commitment? In T. Shibutani (Ed.), *Human nature and collective behavior: Papers in honor of Herbert Blumer* (pp. 18-34). Englewood Cliffs, NJ: Prentice Hall.

Edgerton, R. (1967). *The cloak of competence: Stigma in the lives of the mentally retarded.* Berkeley: University of California Press.

Edgley, C., & Turner, R. E. (1979). On disambiguating Professor Riggs' proposal. *The American Sociologist, 14*, 192-194.

Eichler, M. (1988). *Nonsexist research methods: A practical guide.* Boston: Allen and Unwin.

Ellen, R. F. (Ed.). (1984). *Ethnographic research: A guide to general conduct.* London: Academic Press.

Emmet, D., & MacIntyre, A. (Eds.). (1970). *Sociological theory and philosophical analysis.* London: Macmillan.

The Encyclopedia of Sociology. (1981). Guilford, CT: DPG Reference Publishing.

Falk, R. F., & Anderson, W. D. (1983). Methodological conflicts in symbolic interactionism. *Current Perspectives in Social Theory, 4*, 23-35.

Fine, G. A. (1990). Symbolic interactionism in the post-Blumerian age. In G. Ritzer (Ed.), *Frontiers of social theory: The new synthesis* (pp. 117-157). New York: Columbia University Press.

Fox, R. (1957). Training for uncertainty. In R. K. Merton, G. Reader, & P. L. Kendall (Eds.), *The student physician* (pp. 207-241). Cambridge, MA: Harvard University Press.

Gans, H. J. (1962). *The urban villagers: Group and class in the life of Italian Americans.* Cambridge, MA: Schenkman.

Garfinkle, H. (1956). Conditions of successful degradation ceremonies. *American Journal of Sociology, 61*, 420-424.

Geertz, C. (1983). *Local knowledge: Further essays in interpretive anthropology.* New York: Basic Books.

Geertz, C. (1988). *Works and lives: The anthropologist as author.* Stanford, CA: Stanford University Press.

Gibson, C., MacDonald, H. L., & van den Hoonaard, W. C. (1994). *Partnerships between families of children with asthma and health care professionals: A research proposal presented to the Canadian Nurses' Respiratory Association.* Unpublished manuscript.

Glaser, B., & Strauss, A. (1964). Awareness contexts and social interaction. *American Sociological Review, 29*, 669-679.

Glaser, B., & Strauss, A. (1967). *The discovery of grounded theory: Strategies for qualitative research.* Chicago: Aldine.

Goffman, E. (1959). *Presentation of self in everyday life.* New York: Doubleday Anchor.

Goffman, E. (1961a). *Asylums: Essays on the social situation of mental patients and other inmates.* Garden City, NY: Anchor Doubleday.

Goffman, E. (1961b). *Encounters: Two studies in the sociology of interaction.* Indianapolis, IN: Bobbs-Merrill.

Goffman, E. (1967). *Interaction ritual: Essays on face-to-face behavior.* New York: Pantheon.

Goffman, E. (1971). *Relations in public: Microstudies of the public order.* New York: Harper & Row.

Goffman, E. (1986). *Stigma: Notes on the management of spoiled identity.* New York: Simon & Schuster.

Hammersley, M. (1985). From ethnography to theory: A programme and paradigm in the sociology of education. *Sociology, 19*, 244-259.

80

Hammersley, M. (1989). *The dilemma of qualitative method: Herbert Blumer and the Chicago tradition*. London: Routledge.

Hammersley, M., & Atkinson, P. (1983). *Ethnography: Principles in practice*. London: Tavistock.

Heap, J. L., & Roth, P. A. (1973). On phenomenological sociology. *American Sociological Review, 38*, 354-367.

Hessler, R. M. (1992). *Social research methods*. St. Paul, MN: West.

Hindess, B. (1972). The "phenomenological" sociology of Alfred Schutz. *Economy and Society, 1*, 1-27.

Hochschild, A. R. (1973). *The unexpected community: Portrait of an old age subculture*. Englewood Cliffs, NJ: Prentice Hall.

Hochschild, A. R. (1983). *The managed heart: Commercialization of human feeling*. Berkeley: University of California Press.

Hochschild, A. R. (1989). *The second shift*. New York: Avon.

Hoover, K., & Donovan, T. (1995). *The elements of social scientific thinking* (6th ed.). New York: St. Martin's.

Huber, J. (1973). Symbolic interaction as a pragmatic perspective: The bias of emergent theory. *American Sociological Review, 38*, 274-284.

Hughes, E. C. (1945). Dilemmas and contradictions of status. *American Journal of Sociology, 50*, 353-359.

Humphreys, L. (1970). *Tearoom trade: Impersonal sex in public places*. Chicago: Aldine.

Hutton, K. (1994). *Developing sensitizing concepts*. Unpublished manuscript, Department of Sociology, University of New Brunswick, Fredericton, New Brunswick, Canada.

Kalab, K. A. (1987). Student vocabularies of motive: Accounts for absence. *Symbolic Interaction, 10*, 71-83.

Kirby, S., & McKenna, K. (1989). *Experience, research, social change: Methods from the margins*. Toronto: Garamond.

Klapp, O. (1958). Social types. *American Sociological Review, 23*, 673-681.

Kluckhohn, C. (1985). *Mirror for man*. Tucson: University of Arizona Press. (Original work published 1949)

Lantz, J. C. (1987). *Cumulative index of sociology journals, 1971-1985*. Washington, DC: American Sociological Association.

Levine, D. N. (Ed.). (1971). *Georg Simmel: On individuality and social forms: Selected writings*. Chicago: University of Chicago Press.

Lewis, F., & Stevens, P. (1986). *Iranian refugees in America: A cross-cultural perspective*. Wilmette, IL: United States Bahá'í Refugee Office.

Lewis, J. D. (1976). The classic American pragmatists as forerunners to symbolic interactionism. *Sociological Quarterly, 17*, 346-359.

Lofland, J. (1970). Interactionist imagery and analytic interruptus. In T. Shibutani (Ed.), *Human nature and collective behavior: Papers in honor of Herbert Blumer* (pp. 34-45). Englewood Cliffs, NJ: Prentice Hall.

Lofland, J., & Lofland, L. H. (1984). *Analyzing social settings: A guide to qualitative observation and analysis* (2nd ed.). Belmont, CA: Wadsworth.

Lofland, J., & Lofland, L. H. (1995). *Analyzing social settings: A guide to qualitative observation and analysis* (3rd ed.). Belmont, CA: Wadsworth.

Lopata, H. Z. (1971). *Occupation: Housewife*. New York: Oxford University Press.

Luxton, M. (1980). *More than a labour of love: Three generations of women's work in the home*. Toronto: The Women's Press.

Lyman, S. M., & Vidich, A. J. (1988). *Social order and the public policy: An analysis and interpretation of the work of Herbert Blumer.* Fayetteville: University of Arkansas Press.

Maines, D. R. (1988). Myth, text, and interactionist complicity in the neglect of Blumer's macrosociology. *Symbolic Interaction, 11*, 43-57.

Mann, M. (Ed.). (1983). *The Macmillan student encyclopedia of sociology.* London: Macmillan.

Mannheim, K. (1972). *Ideology and utopia: An introduction to the sociology of knowledge.* London: Routledge & Kegan Paul. (Original work published 1936)

Martindale, D. (1959). Sociological theory and the ideal type. In L. Gross (Ed.), *Symposium on sociological theory* (pp. 57-91). New York: Row, Peterson, and Co.

McCracken, G. (1988). *The long interview.* Newbury Park, CA: Sage.

Mead, G. H. (1962). *Mind, self, and society* (C. W. Morris, Ed.). Chicago: University of Chicago Press. (Original work published 1934)

Merton, R. K. (1938). Social structure and anomie. *American Sociological Review, 3*, 672-682.

Miles, M. B., & Huberman, A. M. (1994). *Qualitative data analysis* (2nd ed.). Thousand Oaks, CA: Sage.

Mills, C. W. (1959). *The sociological imagination.* New York: Grove.

Morgan, D. L. (1988). *Focus groups as qualitative research.* Newbury Park, CA: Sage.

Morrione, T. J. (1988). Herbert G. Blumer (1900-1987): A legacy of concepts, criticisms, and contributions. *Symbolic Interaction, 11*, 1-12.

Needham, R. (1979). *Symbolic classification.* Santa Monica, CA: Goodyear.

Nettler, G. (1970). *Explanations.* New York: McGraw-Hill.

Nielsen, F. (1984). [Review of *Conceptualization and measurement in the social sciences* by Hubert M. Blalock, Jr.]. *American Journal of Sociology, 89*, 1239-1241.

Piercy, M. (1994). *The longings of women.* New York: Fawcett Crest.

Plath, D. W. (1990). Fieldnotes, filed notes, and the conferring of note. In R. Sanjek (Ed.), *Fieldnotes: The makings of anthropology* (pp. 371-384). Ithaca, NY: Cornell University Press.

Portes, A., & Sensenbrenner, J. (1993). Embeddedness and immigration: Notes on the social determinants of economic action. *American Journal of Sociology, 98*, 1320-1350.

Pyke, S. W., & Agnew, N. M. (1991). *The science game: An introduction to research in the social sciences* (5th ed.). Englewood Cliffs, NJ: Prentice Hall.

Ragin, C. C. (1994). *Constructing social research: The unity and diversity of method.* Thousand Oaks, CA: Pine Forge.

Reinharz, S. (1993). *On becoming a social scientist* (4th ed.). New Brunswick, NJ: Transaction.

Reinharz, S., with Davidman, L. (1992). *Feminist methods in social research.* New York: Oxford University Press.

Reynolds, L. T. (1990). *Interactionism: Exposition and critique* (2nd ed.). Dix Hills, NY: General Hall.

Riggs, F. W. (1979). The importance of concepts: Some consideration on how they might be designated less ambiguously. *The American Sociologist, 14*, 172-185.

Roethlisberger, F. J., & Dickson, W. J. (1961). *Management and the worker: An account of a research program conducted by the Western Electric Company, Hawthorne Works, Chicago* (12th ed.). Cambridge, MA: Harvard University Press.

Rowles, G. D., & Reinharz, S. (1988). Qualitative gerontology: Themes and challenges. In S. Reinharz & G. D. Rowles (Eds.), *Qualitative gerontology* (pp. 3-33). New York: Springer.

Sanjek, R. (1990). On ethnographic validity. In R. Sanjek (Ed.), *Fieldnotes: The makings of anthropology* (pp. 385-413). Ithaca, NY: Cornell University Press.

Schama, S. (1987). *The embarrassment of riches: An interpretation of Dutch culture in the golden age.* New York: Knopf.

Schreier, H. A., & Libow, J. A. (1993). *Hurting for love: Munchausen by Proxy Syndrome.* New York: Guilford.

Schulte, J. (1992). *Wittgenstein: An introduction.* Albany: State University of New York Press.

Schutz, A. (1962). *Collected papers: The problem of social reality* (Vol. 1, M. Natanson, Ed.). The Hague: Martinus Nijhoff.

Schutz, A. (1970). Concept and theory formation in the social sciences. In D. Emmet & A. MacIntyre (Eds.), *Sociological theory and philosophical analysis* (pp. 1-19). London: Macmillan.

Schutz, A. (1972). *The phenomenology of the social world.* London: Heinemann.

Shaffir, W. B., Stebbins, R., & Turowetz, A. (Eds.). (1980). *Fieldwork experience: Qualitative approaches to social research.* New York: St. Martin's.

Shibutani, T. (1970). *Human nature and collective behavior: Papers in honor of Herbert Blumer.* Englewood Cliffs, NJ: Prentice Hall.

Shibutani, T. (1988). Herbert Blumer: Contributions to 20th Century sociology. *Symbolic Interaction, 11,* 23-31.

Sjoberg, G., & Nett, R. (1968). *A methodology for social research.* New York: Harper and Row.

Smith, H. W. (1991). *Strategies of social research* (3rd ed.). Fort Worth, TX: Holt, Rinehart & Winston.

Smith, H. W. (1994). Doing stand-up: Comedians on stage. In M. L. Dietz, R. Prus, & W. Shaffir (Eds.), *Doing everyday life: Ethnography as human lived experience* (pp. 245-259). Misssisauga, Ontario, Canada: Copp Clark Longman.

Stebbins, R. A. (1990). *Sociology: The study of society* (2nd ed.). Grand Rapids, MI: Harper and Row.

Strauss, A. L. (1987). *Qualitative analysis for social scientists.* Cambridge, UK: Cambridge University Press.

Strauss, A. L., Fagerhaugh, S., Suczek, B., & Wiener, C. (1985). *The social organization of medical work.* Chicago: University of Chicago Press.

Stryker, S. (1988). Substance and style: An appraisal of the sociological legacy of Herbert Blumer. *Symbolic Interaction, 11,* 33-42.

Truzzi, M. (Ed.). (1974). *Verstehen: Subjective understanding in the social sciences.* Reading, MA: Addison-Wesley.

Tucker, C. W. (1988). Herbert Blumer: A pilgrimage with pragmatism. *Symbolic Interaction, 11,* 99-124.

Turner, J. H. (1978). Symbolic interactionism and social organization. In J. G. Manis & B. N. Meltzer (Eds.), *Symbolic interaction: A reader in social psychology* (3rd ed., pp. 400-402). Boston: Allyn & Bacon.

Turner, L. (1994). *Discovering and developing sensitizing concepts.* Unpublished manuscript, Department of Sociology, University of New Brunswick, Fredericton, New Brunswick, Canada.

Udy, S. H., Jr. (1964). Cross-cultural analysis: A case study. In P. Hammond (Ed.), *Sociologists at work* (pp. 161-183). New York: Basic Books.

Unruh, D. R. (1983). *Invisible lives.* Beverly Hills, CA: Sage.

van den Hoonaard, D. K. (1995a). *A different life: Life histories of widows.* Unpublished manuscript.

van den Hoonaard, D. K. (1995b). *Identity foreclosure: Women's experiences of widowhood as expressed in autobiographical accounts.* Unpublished manuscript.

van den Hoonaard, W. C. (1972). *Local-level autonomy: A case study of an Icelandic fishing community.* Unpublished master's thesis, Department of Sociology and Anthropology, Memorial University of Newfoundland, St. John's, Newfoundland, Canada.

van den Hoonaard, W. C. (1991). *Silent ethnicity: The Dutch of New Brunswick.* Fredericton, New Brunswick, Canada: New Ireland Press.

van den Hoonaard, W. C. (1992). *Reluctant pioneers: Constraints and opportunities in an Icelandic fishing community.* New York: Peter Lang.

van den Hoonaard, W. C. (1996, May). *A "new ethnography" in an old field setting: Iceland.* Paper presented at the Qualitative Analysis Conference, McMaster University, Hamilton, Ontario.

Van Maanen, J. (1988). *Tales of the field: On writing ethnography.* Chicago: University of Chicago Press.

Warshay, L. H., & Warshay, D. W. (1986). The individualizing and subjectivizing of George Herbert Mead: A sociology of knowledge interpretation. *Sociological Focus, 19,* 177-188.

Weber, M. (1949). *The methodology of the social sciences.* Trans. by E. A. Shils & H. A. Finch. Glencoe, IL: Free Press.

Weber, M. (1964). *The theory of social and economic organization.* New York: Free Press.

Wellman, D. (1988). The politics of Herbert Blumer's sociological method. *Symbolic Interaction, 11,* 59-68.

Whittaker, E. (1994). The contribution of Herbert Blumer to anthropology. In M. L. Dietz, R. Prus, & W. Shaffir (Eds.), *Doing everyday life: Ethnography as human lived experience* (pp. 379-392). Misssisauga, Ontario, Canada: Copp Clark Longman.

Zerubavel, E. (1980). If Simmel were a fieldworker: On formal sociological theory and analytical field research. *Symbolic Interaction, 3,* 25-33.

Zimmerman, M. A., & Arunkumar, R. (1994). Resiliency research: Implications for schools and policy. *Social Policy Report, 8,* 1-18.

ABOUT THE AUTHOR

WILL C. van den HOONAARD is Professor of Sociology at the University of New Brunswick in Fredericton, New Brunswick, Canada. He has authored several books, including *Silent Ethnicity: The Dutch of New Brunswick* (1991), *Reluctant Pioneers: Constraints and Opportunities in an Icelandic Fishing Community* (1992), and *The Origins of the Bahá'í Community in Canada, 1898-1948* (forthcoming). Eclectic and diverse in his approach, he has published or presented some 70 papers in the areas of social movements, ethnic relations, the sociology of Georg Simmel, the social organization of airports, chaos theory, demography, and qualitative research methods. Dr. van den Hoonaard is a Woodrow Wilson Fellow (1970) and has won several awards, including the "Excellence in Bahá'í Studies" offered by the international Association for Bahá'í Studies. He is currently President of the Atlantic Association of Sociologists and Anthropologists and Editor of the *Newsbulletin* of the Executive Board of the Association for the Advancement of Scandinavian Studies in Canada. Dr. van den Hoonaard spent his school years in France, Canada, and the Netherlands, and he obtained his PhD in sociology at the University of Manchester, England.

Qualitative Research Methods

Series Editor
JOHN VAN MAANEN
Massachusetts Institute of Technology

Associate Editors:
Peter K. Manning, *Michigan State University*
& Marc L. Miller, *University of Washington*

Other volumes in this series listed on outside back cover